A WORD IN SEASON

Jan 10, 1993

Micah,
 I have been so thankful for your life and desire to serve Him. May you always want to please the Lord.
  Love always,
   Dad

CHET PLIMPTON

LC LONGWOOD COMMUNICATIONS

Copyright © 1993 by Chet Plimpton

All rights reserved
Printed in the United States of America
International Standard Book Number: 0-9632190-4-9
Library of Congress Catalog Card Number: 93-078051

This book or parts thereof may not be reproduced in any form without permission of the author.

Unless otherwise noted, all Scripture quotations are from the King James Version of the Bible. Personal emphasis, noted by italics, has also been added in various verses.

Published by:
Longwood Communications
397 Kingslake Drive
DeBary, FL 32713
904-774-1991

Dedication

It is a joy to dedicate this book to my wife, Anita, who has countless times been used of God to speak that "word in season" to my heart.

A Word in Season

Contents

Preface 7
Foreword 9
1. To Him That Is Weary 11
2. In Pursuit of Promotion 19
3. Running the Race 27
4. A Word to Shepherds 35
5. Dealing With Hurt 40
6. A Call to Faithfulness 50
7. A Vessel Unto Honour 57
8. Are You Successful? 61
9. Remember to Encourage 65
10. Our Spiritual Perspective 72
11. What Is Your Duty Status? 81
12. Conflict! 86
13. Spiritual Reality 93
14. In Someone's Thoughts 100
15. Strengthen What Remains 108
16. Listening 116
17. Gateways Into The Heart 127
18. The Greed of Gehazi 136
19. Purity Is Priority 143
20. Let There Be No Strife 150
21. Choosing Thankfulness 157
22. Provisions of Grace 164
23. Aspects of Conformity 179
24. Keep It Simple 191
    Scripture Index 202

A Word in Season

Preface

The title of this book is borrowed from that portion of Isaiah 50:4 which reads, "a word in season to him that is weary." In past years God has allowed my wife and me a very small part in preparing men and women for missionary work and in encouraging them after they have faithfully served in the thick of the battle. It is from these efforts that the contents of this book first originated, in the form of teaching notes and articles. Of course it is not only missionaries who become weary; all of us experience weariness of many kinds, and we all need encouragement to keep focused on the Lord and upon His Word. Sometimes a word spoken (or read!) can be just what we need to help us to walk in a way pleasing to God.

A Word in Season

When David, in great anger and with his sword at his side, went to destroy Nabal, Abigail met him with a "word in season" that stopped him in his tracks. Through this woman's timely words, David was kept from taking matters into his own hands or leaning on his own wisdom.

Encouraged with the fact that God uses little things like this woman's words and the "widow's mite," we pass these simple Bible studies on to you as a missionary, full-time worker, or as a believer in Jesus Christ, trusting and praying that God will use them to direct your thoughts to His Word, which might be that "word in season" to your heart.

Foreword

"I will greatly rejoice in the Lord, my soul shall be joyful in my God; for he hath clothed me with the garments of salvation, he hath covered me with the robe of righteousness..." (Isa. 61:10).

It is emptiness to try to find lasting joy or fulfillment in the things of this world. Our hearts are sometimes drawn toward material security, life's pleasures, or our accomplishments, only to be disappointed with their inability to satisfy us. We are like a hungry boy who, after staring longingly at the cookie jar high on the shelf, reaches his hand in only to grab a few broken pieces and scattered crumbs. But rejoice! There is One who can fill the emptiness of your heart and satisfy every longing of your soul. He is the One who clothed you with salvation and covered you with righteousness, at great cost and with matchless grace. Only He is our true source of joy.

My Only Joy
Thy blood hast flowed in mercy free
Thy heart's desire to ransom me.
Could my heart crave for else but Thee,
When Thou hast longed for such as me?

Thine anguish was the prospect grim,
That Holiness should bear my sin.
Could I so live to bring Thee pain,
When Thy soul bore such awful stain?

Thy voice cried out as darkness raced,
And hid from Thee Thy Father's face.
How could I turn my eyes from Thee,
When Thou had lost His gaze for me?

Thy grace dissolves my own poor claim,
To chart my course, to praise my name,
How can I seek ought else but Thee,
When Thou hast shown such grace to me?

O God, my only joy can be,
To walk in fellowship with Thee.
When countless ages round me roll,
I'll gladly serve Thee heart and soul!

Chapter One

TO HIM THAT IS WEARY

"The Lord GOD hath given me the
tongue of the learned, that I should know
how to speak a word in season to him
that is weary" (Isa. 50:4).

We have gained a lot of know-how in many areas. Those in mission organizations will testify that we have learned to do many things. We can build computers and operate them; we can fly planes and overhaul them; we can break down languages and translate the Scriptures into them, to name just a few accomplishments. However, we all have an ongoing need to gain "know how" in simply encouraging those who are weary! This know-how cannot be gained by going to school or taking a course in psychology or counseling. It is not something that can be assigned to anyone in particular as a ministry or job description, and it must never be considered as a task only select people can do.

The source of all true encouragement is God Himself as Isaiah confesses, "The Lord God hath given..." It is God alone who gives His servants the sensitivity and ability to speak His words, and it is God alone who uses His Word to lift the hearts of those who are weary.

We all find ourselves at both ends of this verse — at times we will be the ones who encourage the weary, and other times we will be the weary who need encouragement.

Two things are important to understand when we consider weariness and the believer: Satan's intention and God's victory. An awareness of these two things will serve as a foundation under our feet when we are weary or when we are encouraging others who are weary.

Satan's Intention

It has always been the intention of Satan to express hatred and rejection of God by attacking God's people. Daniel told of the character of the anti-Christ of the last days in these words: "And he shall speak great words against the most High, and shall wear out the saints of the most High" (Dan. 7:25). The actual meaning of the words *wear out* leaves us with no doubt as to the intention of Satan. The meaning is "to persecute with the purpose of entire annihilation."

It is not simply to tire us out but to destroy us altogether! Although Satan has designed his world's system to annihilate God's people, his real intent has always been to taunt God and exalt himself as equal with God. In Isaiah 14:14 we read this account of his intention: "I will be like the most High."

God's Victory

All of Satan's intentions to frustrate God's purposes and rob God of glory are doomed to failure as

To Him That Is Weary

Isaiah 14:15 says: "Yet thou shalt be brought down to hell." Satan's intent to annihilate God's people has also been doomed to failure from the start. An illustration of this is found in 1 Kings 19. During the wicked reign of Ahab and Jezebel it seemed to many, including the prophet Elijah, that all of God's people had been wiped out. Twice Elijah said to God, "I, even I only, am left; and they seek my life, to take it away" (1 Kings 19:10,14). Later, God cleared up Elijah's wrong thinking by saying, "Yet I have left me seven thousand in Israel, all the knees which have not bowed unto Baal, and every mouth which hath not kissed him" (1 Kings 19:18). Also, during this age in which we live, God is adding people to His church despite the attempts of Satan and this world to prevent it. Jesus said, "I will build my church; and the gates of hell shall not prevail against it" (Matt. 16:18).

In all this there is the clear ring of victory echoing down the mountaintops of the ages. It must be remembered, however, that the victory belongs to God alone. We enter into His victory. "For he is our God; and we are the people of his pasture, and the sheep of his hand" (Ps. 95:7). How secure to be positioned in His pasture! We cannot be separated from His love and care, no matter how weary we become. It is when we realize we cannot hold on, that we know He is holding on to us. When we realize we do not have strength to keep ourselves, it is then we know that He is keeping us. It is essential to have this truth as an anchor for our souls when we are weary or just plain worn out.

When we are weary, we sometimes identify our tiredness with terms such as *tuckered out, stressed out,* and *worn out.*

Tuckered Out

There is the weariness that comes to each of us

simply because of the physical exertion required to accomplish our tasks. We cannot escape this and should accept it as a natural result of giving ourselves to serving God and others. God's servants constantly live with a certain degree of physical weariness. In almost all our areas of ministry we could use more help, so it is not difficult to see the problem! Many believers are carrying more than the work load of one person!

We should be especially careful to give our bodies rest and not drive them thoughtlessly to the point of physical exhaustion. We must also be alert to the needs of others in this respect and not make light of their weariness. A missionary newly arrived on the field often becomes weary quickly, because of the stresses of heat, travel, and change. It would be very insensitive for a missionary somewhat accustomed to living in that situation to comment, "If you think you're tired now, just wait..."

Jesus was not a stranger to physical weariness and no doubt felt it often. In John 4:6 we read, "Jesus therefore, being wearied with his journey, sat thus on the well." The simple fact that Jesus sat on the well shows that He was mindful of taking a few moments to rest so that He could then continue to do His Father's will. This is an important principle that each of us must try to apply reasonably to our own situations of health and work. Our problem is that we tend to be unreasonable, either by taking on too much work or seeking too much ease and comfort. Also, we do not seem to stay alert to the needs of others for rest. Philippians 2:4 says, "Look not every man on his own things, but every man also on the things of others." As husbands and as wives we should be very conscious of how our mates are faring and try to be very understanding and supportive. As believers we should pray for one another and offer help and encouraging words. As leaders we must be mindful of the work load people carry, and we should be careful that they are not overloaded, even though they seem willing to shoulder any task.

Stressed Out

There is the weariness that comes upon us because of the trials and troubles we experience as we seek to live in ways pleasing to God. In 2 Corinthians 11:27 Paul recounted the many difficulties he faced as he served the Lord and spoke of being "in weariness... often." The word *weariness* seems to speak of exhaustion that is the result of working very hard under the stressful conditions of persecutions or trials of some kind. As we look at the list of troubles Paul went through continually, we have no difficulty understanding his weariness. He traveled much and was continually in danger from robbers who would seek to kill him for what they could get from him, and Jews who would kill him out of hatred because of his faith in Christ. Paul's life was at risk as he traveled over sea and through the wilderness. He had already felt the whip, been beaten, thrown in prison, and lost at sea. He had gone hungry and thirsty and had shivered in the cold.

Many missionaries face the daily uncertainty of not knowing whether their lives will be in danger because of guerrilla activity or the efforts of the enemies of the gospel.

The possibility of being taken as a hostage or forced to leave the tribe they are working in is very real. Paul knew this uncertainty well. In Damascus the governor wanted to capture him, and Paul had to flee quickly. He said, "Through a window in a basket was I let down by the wall, and escaped his hands" (2 Cor. 11:33). In Antioch certain Jews stirred up the anger of people against Paul and Barnabas and "expelled them out of their coasts" (Acts 13:50). No doubt if there had been newspapers, radio, and television, these Jews would have used them to spread false accusations and misleading headlines throughout the region.

When we think of what Paul experienced and what believers serving God today experience, we realize the enemy hasn't changed his approach much in almost 2,000 years. He would bring weariness upon us in an attempt to wear us out altogether.

Worn Out

It is when we are weary that we seem to have a desperate need for understanding and comfort, and it is when others are weary that we often fail them by a lack of kindness and tenderness. Without saying these exact words, many times as weary believers we cry out, "Please understand!"

The problem is, when someone is weary it does not always show, at least at a casual glance, and tragically, that is often all we give one another. Sometimes we seem to have little patience with tired people and speak or act unkindly when they really need an encouraging word. We have no idea how much our unkindness and insensitivity hurts others who are weary, and if they finally quit because of discouragement, we shake our heads and wonder how some people can have such a lack of dedication and commitment!

If we pride ourselves in our own dedication and progress yet lack basic kindness to others, are we really pleasing God? First Corinthians 13 tells us that we can possess many gifts and accomplish great things, yet if we lack love, we are missing the mark. Verse 4 says, "Love is kind"(NIV). Is it demonstrated in our lives? We have the opportunity to be used of the

Lord to gently but consistently encourage others to keep trusting God. Jonathan, Saul's son, put his own life at considerable risk when he went to David, who was hiding from Saul and was extremely weary. First Samuel 23:16 says, "And Jonathan Saul's son arose, and went to David into the wood, and strengthened his hand in God."

Physical weariness and the weariness of trials and troubles make a deadly combination. Bleach is strong and ammonia is stronger, but if you were to mix the two the resulting fumes could kill you quickly. Believers who are worn out physically and also worn out with emotional stress are in a very vulnerable condition. This is the favorite time for the enemy to attack with his final blow or fatal stroke.

An excellent illustration of this is the story of David, who in extreme weariness and confusion of disorientation, was fleeing from his own son Absalom who had conspired to take the throne. Absalom's counselor, Ahithophel, portrayed the vicious attitude and objective of our ENEMY when he said to Absalom, "Let me now choose out twelve thousand men, and I will arise and pursue after David this night: and I will come upon him while he is weary and weak handed, and will make him afraid: and all the people that are with him shall flee; and I will smite the king only" (2 Sam. 17:1-2).

God intervened for David at this crucial point in his life and used Hushai, David's friend, to convince Absalom to wait. We are safe in our position, seated with Christ in His place of victory. God will intervene for you and me likewise. He will never leave us or forsake us, which means He will not abandon us or leave us helpless (see Heb. 13:5).

In Due Season

Ecclesiastes 3:1 says, "To every thing there is a season," or an appointed time. Galatians 6:9 says, "And let us not be weary in well doing: for in due season we shall reap, if we faint not." God has appointed a time when our service of love to Him will bear results to His eternal glory. It is one thing to start out doing well, but it is another thing to keep on doing well when weariness settles upon us. The words *be weary* were used to speak of farmers who stopped working hard and diligently because their continual labors had taken a toll on their strength and determination. The result would be their "fainting," or being overcome and exhausted altogether, thus losing the harvest.

Of course, unlike the farmer, we have the joy of drawing upon the strength of another. In fact, we have the privilege of exchanging our feebleness for the inexhaustible resources of strength of the Creator Himself! God Himself can never become weary, as Isaiah 40:28 says: "Hast thou not known? hast thou not heard, that the everlasting God, the Lord, the Creator of the ends of the earth, fainteth not, neither is weary?" Although we are very weak and have absolutely no resources in ourselves to draw upon, when we trust only in God, He applies His own inexhaustible strength as Creator to our weakness as creatures. Isaiah 40:31 says it this way: "But they that wait upon the Lord shall renew their strength (exchange their weakness for His strength); they shall mount up with wings as eagles; they shall run, and not be weary; they shall walk, and not faint."

To him that is weary...wait upon the Lord!

Chapter Two

IN PURSUIT OF PROMOTION

"And seekest thou great things for thyself? seek them not" (Jer. 45:5).

These words of God unto Baruch have spoken to my own heart many times. What is my answer to this question? Am I seeking my own promotion, glory, or praise? What *really* matters to me? Is it that I be recognized for my worth, accomplishments, and efforts, or do I sincerely care nothing for all that and care only that He is pleased and glorified and that His will is done?

The promotion of self has been the cause of much conflict and jealousy since the beginning of time. It remains as one of the chief contributing causes of problems and casualties among missionaries. Even more tragic than this, however, is that if my heart is given to promoting myself, it is robbing from God what truly belongs only to Him. Self-promotion is a form of idolatry.

The following seven "case studies" from Scripture deal with self-promotion. You may not see yourself in all these scenarios, but it is amazing to me how much I can identify with the struggles these people endured as they sought great things for themselves.

Saul — Threatened by a Co-worker (1 Sam. 18:5-9)

There was a time when Saul valued having David around. After all, David had demonstrated courage and confidence in God by standing up to Goliath, and Saul had given David more and more responsibility, which David handled wisely and successfully. It was obvious that God was blessing David and was glorifying Himself. So far Saul had no problem because it didn't seem that David was a threat to his own self-esteem. However, the problem began when Saul heard the women singing! We read in verse 8, "And Saul was very wroth, and the saying displeased him." What saying made Saul so angry? "Saul hath slain his thousands, and David his ten thousands" (v. 7). Saul, in bitterness and resentment said, "They have ascribed unto David ten thousands, and to me they have ascribed but thousands: and what can he have more but the kingdom?" Our self-seeking attitude is often betrayed by the pangs of jealousy and resentment we feel when we hear others crediting our co-workers for accomplishments and successes. This is especially true when our own accomplishments seem to go unnoticed while others get "full-page coverage." This was one of those crossroads in Saul's life. We all have them — times when our choices determine our destiny. Saul could have humbled himself and rejoiced that God could use his life to slay thousands of the enemy, if not tens of thousands. But he chose instead to "eye David from that day and forward" (v. 9). He turned against

David in his heart and chose a relationship of suspicion and mistrust. Such fleshly relationships among us as missionaries are responsible for many wasted resources of time, money, and energy. The time and energy that Saul expended in keeping an eye on David could have been wisely invested in keeping an eye on kingdom matters and the enemy. Because of his foolish pride, Saul saw his most valuable and devoted servant as a hated competitor. Is there anyone that you are "eyeing"? Is there anyone that you feel threatened by? If so, perhaps you are at that crossroad of choice. Be sure you choose the path of humility.

Diotrephes — Not a Team Player (3 John 9-11)

Our eagerness to promote ourselves can be very costly to our ministry in the work of God. Diotrephes refused to have Paul and other believers minister in his pulpit. Diotrephes did not believe in the function of the body. He was not a team player. The work of God suffered because of his love for personal control and recognition. How much blessing to that local church — and opportunity for spiritual growth among them as individuals — was forfeited because Diotrephes had chosen to seek great things for himself? Perhaps Diotrephes was like many in Christian ministry today who claim to be zealous for God's work and determined not to allow any intrusion of wrong teaching or emphasis, when in actuality they are protecting their little empires that they have determined should bring glory to them! May God help us to recognize and deal with any such selfish inclinations! How would love of preeminence show up in our lives? Are we unwilling to allow others to have input into the specific work we are doing such as teaching, translating, keeping the culture file, or medical work? And are we protective of our projects?

Undoubtedly, Diotrephes was a very touchy individual. He certainly was not approachable and was difficult to work with. How about you and me? Are we touchy, unapproachable, insistent upon our own way?

Miriam and Aaron — Faultfinding (Num. 12:1-2)

Some people thrive under leadership while others chafe. What makes the difference? Undoubtedly, the quality of leadership has something to do with it. However, the attitude of the one being led is the most deciding factor. If my heart is set to please God and glorify Him, then I will recognize and appreciate His direction through imperfect human vessels. My attitude toward leaders would then be supportive, constructive, and always helpful, even when I must share a concern or disagreement. On the other hand, problems develop when I don't approve of those who have been appointed to lead, and I am grasping after a leadership position for myself. We can identify this as "power-seeking" and it is, perhaps, what Miriam and Aaron were caught up in. They obviously did not approve of the woman their brother married. They simply could not reconcile in their minds how anyone who would marry a woman like that could be a leader in Israel! How can we apply this personally to ourselves? Perhaps we could attempt to fill in the missing phrase in the following sentence: "How can anyone who... be a leader in our mission organization or an elder in our church?" If our heart attitude is one of power-seeking and self-promotion, then we are all too quick to disqualify certain people from holding leadership positions. Miriam and Aaron became very bold and self-assertive. Their claim was that they had been around as long as Moses and knew the mind of God for Israel just as well as Moses did! They said,

"...Hath the Lord indeed spoken only by Moses? hath he not spoken also by us?" (v. 2).

May God help each of us to have a mind-set to serve Him faithfully for many years without requiring a position or recognition because of longevity. It has been a great personal blessing to talk with people who have been in God's service for thirty or forty years but have no personal aspirations; they are only rejoicing for the years of service God has given them.

The Twelve Disciples — Looking for Position
(Mark 9:33-37; Matt. 18:1; Luke 9:46; 22:24)

"Then there arose a reasoning among them, which of them should be greatest" (Luke 9:46). How blind these twelve men were to their situation! They were, after all, mere men, called from various humble walks of life to follow Christ. From pulling in nets loaded with fishes to collecting unpaid taxes, they really had nothing to boast about. Yet in their very presence was the One who was truly great and wonderful. Even the apostle Paul, who was highly educated and had power and authority given him, considered all his personal potential and attainments to be of absolutely no value when compared to knowing and worshiping the Lord Jesus Christ. Does it give us secret satisfaction to think that we are the main cause, the recognized authority in our field, the leader of the group — that things just would not go as smoothly if we were not in the tribe, in the school, in the dorm, or in the office? It is wrong to desire personal greatness. Galatians 5:26 says, "Let us not be desirous of vain glory." If we desire personal greatness, we are blind to at least two fundamental facts. First, when we pursue glory for ourselves, we are passing up the opportunity to bring glory to the only true great One. Second, like the disciples, we really have nothing to get excited about when we consider our own personal potential for greatness. Paul wrote that we should not elevate ourselves over others because we have absolutely no potential that God did not give us; if all we have was given to us, why should we boast as though we had earned it, as if we were somehow inherently better than others? "What hast thou that thou didst not receive? now if thou didst receive it, why dost thou glory, as if thou hadst not received it?" (1 Cor. 4:7).

The Twelve versus James and John — Unwilling to Serve Others (Mark 10:35-45)

"...Grant unto us that we may sit, one on thy right hand, and the other on thy left hand, in thy glory" (v. 37).

We don't know the motive behind this request of these two brothers, James and John, but we certainly know what the reaction of the other ten disciples was! "And when the ten heard it, they began to be much displeased with James and John" (v. 41). How it upsets us when we think that our co-workers are trying to establish themselves in some place of prominence or responsibility by being very friendly or by trying to convince home or field leadership of their qualifications! However, this resentment and irritation on our part exposes our own heart condition of wanting great things for ourselves! Why else would we become upset at others who seem set on promoting themselves? This situation provided a perfect opportunity for Jesus to teach His disciples what true greatness is in a child of God. Greatness, as the world knows it, means being top dog, boss, director, president, the highest paid, the committee member, etc. However, true greatness is simply to serve and minister to others. The greatest Man of all came to earth purposefully to minister to us and to give His life for us. Christ never sought a position or an office; in fact, Philippians 2:7 says that He "made Himself of no reputation." He emptied Himself in order to assume the form of a servant. Will we allow God to bring us to the point of letting go of our inner strivings to be someone of importance?

Euodias and Syntyche — Poles Apart in Opinions (Phil. 4:2)

"I beseech Euodias, and beseech Syntyche, that they be of the same mind in the Lord." This represents one of the chief difficulties believers face in working together. At times opinions can seem poles apart and decisions out of reach. The struggles we face in not being of the same mind as our co-workers are a result of attitudes we hold toward them personally. Perhaps a co-worker threatens or intimidates us, or perhaps he or she seems strong or forceful in expressing opinions. We fear that if we don't watch out, this person will take over. It is easy then for us to dig our heels in and set ourselves in opposition, not so much to their thoughts and opinions but to them personally.

Perhaps this was the problem these two ladies were facing. Paul simply pleaded with them to *choose* to deal with their attitudes and be in fellowship with the Lord and each other. After all, as the verse explains, likemindedness is in the Lord.

Peter — Unrestful and Anxious (John 21:19-22)

"...Lord, and what shall this man do?" (v. 21).

Jesus had just given Peter very clear instructions: "Follow me" (v. 19); yet Peter, like many of us, just couldn't let the matter rest there. He simply had to know what the Lord's plans were for John. Perhaps Peter was concerned that everything was going to be fair. We don't really know, of course, what motives were behind Peter's question, but we do know that in answering him, Jesus repeated His clear instructions, "follow... me" (v. 22), along with an exhortation that whatever His plans were for John, they didn't affect His plans for Peter in any way. Usually, when we are anxious to know what is going to happen with others, we also have many "how come" questions: How come they are gone so often? How come the Committee asked them to work in that tribe? How come they get extra vacation time? Many times "how come" questions only muddy the waters of our own understanding and acceptance of God's will for us. At times we feel that it is not right that others seem to take advantage of liberties and lack a sense of responsibility to their ministry and co-workers. This could be the case, and we could find bitterness in our hearts over it. However, if we were not concerned that others get ahead of us in promotion or privilege, or if we did not react to others' behavior, we would probably only hear the words "follow me," and those words would fill our hearts with thankfulness and anticipation.

Your Name: _____ — Having Choices to Make

What can we do if we have come to realize that our hearts struggle for self-promotion? We began our study thinking of God's question to Jeremiah, "Seekest thou great things for thyself?" We conclude by saying that God responded to His own question with the words, "Seek them not." We have a choice in all this! We don't have to seek great things for ourselves. We can choose instead to live to please and glorify our wonderful Lord.

Chapter Three

RUNNING THE RACE

"Now they do it to obtain a corruptible
crown; but we an incorruptible"
(1 Cor. 9:25).

One of the most enjoyable things Anita and I have done is to go to various races and cross-country meets that our children have taken part in. We thought you might enjoy "going with us" to some of the meets our daughter, Jessica, ran in, and consider with us some practical applications to our own Christian lives.

What Will the Finish Line Reveal?

One of the most moving moments of a race is at the finish line, watching the faces of the runners as they complete the last few meters. Etched into these faces is the story of the race — hopes, disappointments, determination, and physical exhaustion.

Before the starter's gun fires, the runners mingle,

laughing or perhaps even discussing the upcoming race. However, when you look deeply into their faces at the finish line, you are struck with the reality that each has run his own individual race. Each had to cover the necessary ground a step at a time. We have watched our own children's faces and together with them, we have watched the faces of other runners as they strained to the finish. Faces of exhausted runners are not the most attractive, except to those who understand and appreciate all that a runner must go through from start to finish.

Our society is foolishly concerned about covering up the lines and signs of age and the evidence of having lived life. The cosmetic business is booming over sale of paste and paint. However, Paul wrote, " I bear in my body the marks of the Lord Jesus" (Gal. 6:17). Everything about Paul showed that he had lived unreservedly for God. His body showed the scars of persecution and the evidence of suffering. His life testified to the faithfulness of God, who supplied all that Paul needed.

Eventually, each of us will approach the last few meters of our race. Will our lives glorify God before those watching us reach the finish line? Will they see, etched in our lives, a joyful expectation of being with Him and a determination to give all for love of Him?

Can You Run Without Shoes?

It had rained recently and the runners' course was wet and slippery. To make matters worse, there were muddy areas that were difficult to avoid without losing precious time. As Jessica came into sight, heading toward the finish line, it was obvious that her mother would have an especially challenging wash day that week! Hadn't Jessica begun the race with running shoes? Why was she sprinting toward the finish line in very muddy socks? It wasn't very complicated, really. Going through a muddy place, she had heard a sucking sound. A glance confirmed that one running shoe was not going to finish the race; it was firmly stuck in the mud. She had no time to lose going back for it, and running cross-country with only one shoe can be worse than running with none. One quick movement and the other shoe rested beside the course, waiting to be picked up with its mate when the race was over.

Do you need shoes to finish a race? They are a great help for traction as well as safety, but there are times when you might have to leave them behind to avoid losing precious time. Even good and helpful things sometimes become a hindrance to finishing the race in which God has entered us. We hang on to good things like equipment, relationships, proper exercise, and diet, when we should let go of our possessive grip on these things and just continue on "shoeless." It is good to learn how to run with shoes or without shoes! Paul wrote in Philippians 4:11-13:

"I have learned, in whatsoever state I am, therewith to be content. I know both how to be abased, and I know how to abound ... I can do all things through Christ which strengtheneth me."

Running With a Friend

Running with a friend has definite advantages; two especially stand out. When Jessica first started running cross-country, she had the determination and the ability to run but didn't understand how to pace herself. Of course, a long-distance runner cannot sprint all the way but might pour on extra speed for a few meters at the start and again near the finish line. Jessica's friend Jodi helped her to learn how hard to push herself so she did not use up her energy too quickly.

Sometimes capable, gifted missionaries get

disheartened and are a source of discouragement to others because they involve themselves in their work to the exclusion of spending quality time with their families. They are like runners who try to sprint all the way, not understanding that some of their energies must be directed to mates and children who desperately need them but cannot get their attention as they flash by. Let's encourage those running close to us in the race by making sure they do not feel pressured to run at top speed all the time and that they take time to be at home.

Cross-country meets are seldom canceled. No matter what the weather or temperature, the race goes on. At times, it is very hard for a runner to get enthusiastic about running, much less do his or her very best. One afternoon as we joined others to watch the race it was raining, and the air was a teeth-chattering cold. We got there too late for the starting gun but saw the runners as they went by on their first loop and, finally, at the finish. What interested us was the sight of Jessica and Tracy running side by side, encouraging each other on by simply being together. They both did well, no doubt partly because each had a friend running alongside.

There are days for each of us when we just don't feel like running. Paul expressed the importance of believers running together in Hebrews 10:24 — "And let us consider one another to provoke unto love and to good works."

Confusion on the Course

It was another wet fall day, and the ski hills of Chickopee were both steep and slippery. It was going to be a grueling 3,200-meter run! To make matters worse, our school's bus was not any too early getting to Chickopee, and the runners had yet to walk the course to familiarize themselves with it. I asked the coach if there was anything I could do! Because he needed to attend a coaches' meeting, he asked me if I would take the runners for a quick walk of the course. It's true that we had a little map to follow, but about halfway through we got mixed up and were not sure where to go. We knew one thing; the intermediate girls were to run soon, and we scrambled to get back to the starting line before the race began. I can still remember us running down the first hill toward the hundreds of intermediate girls already lined up to begin the race. I felt terrible that our girls didn't know the entire course, but I guess there were many others who didn't have a chance to walk the course either.

Jessica's face was a picture of concentration as she took her place among the runners. She had not complained about not being able to walk the entire course, and I knew she was determined to do her best and keep the leaders in sight. There is something stirring in the contrast between watching hundreds of runners bunched together at the starting line and then cheering them at the finish, no longer in a mass but strung out, working hard to gain a place or two or perhaps simply to finish. Here Jessica came, number thirteen! We were exuberant! Of the nearly four hundred runners who started, about one hundred never finished the entire course — partly because of the grueling hills and partly because the course had not been previously traveled and runners became confused and discouraged.

It made me think of Hebrews 12:1-2 — "Let us run with patience the race that is set before us, looking unto Jesus the author and finisher of our faith." We have a God who knows every inch of our life's course. It is absolutely vital to keep our eyes upon Him and not become confused when Satan seeks to distract us by his countless evil devices. Somehow Jessica was able to concentrate on the race set before her—to keep her eyes on the leaders who had previously run the course. Life can quickly become an impossible maze if we do not continue to trust and obey God *step by step*. Some runners gave up on the hills because it was very tough going. Hills may look impossible when you stand at the bottom and look up, but they can be conquered one step at a time. If we want to finish our race, we must run it with patience and endurance, determined at the starting line that by God's grace we will finish and not give up.

You're Not Finished Until You're Finished!

As she passed by on the first lap, we saw that Jessica was in fifth place. As she disappeared again into the woods, we were cheering her on and hoping she could hold that place or maybe gain one. Now she was coming into view and yes, she had a solid grip on fourth place! She would definitely place fourth, as the girl behind her could not possibly gain enough ground to pass her. The finish line was marked by a set of pylons in a funnel shape, with the actual finish line at the far, narrow end. Yes, there she was, entering the funnel, only seconds now between her and the finished race! But why was she stopping just inside the funnel? She had thought that the finish line was at the funnel's beginning, not the end! Momentarily speechless, we silently urged her to run all the way through. Suddenly, she seemed to realize her mistake and made a desperate effort to correct her error — just as the fifth-place runner went by her to come in fourth! We shared her disappointment but sincerely congratulated her in a good race. However, the lesson was too important to miss, and we learned it together. Our race isn't finished until it is finished!

How many Christians have served God faithfully

for many years only to fall into a life of sin right at the "mouth of the funnel"! The Enemy will seek to do us spiritual harm until we cross the finish line, beyond which he can no longer influence us. How important it is to guard our hearts from bitterness, unbelief, and evil thoughts over every step of the race. How tragic it would be to have years of preparation behind us, the tribal language learned, the teaching begun, and then stop just short of completing the job. No wonder that Paul, when comparing the Christian life to a race said, "So run, that ye may obtain" (1 Cor. 9:24).

The *How* and the *Why* of the Race

There have been many colored ribbons and medals brought home from Jessica's races, but interestingly enough, the most meaningful have not always been those for first place. It is not so important to be first over the line; what *is* important is how and why the race was run. Few people wait around the finish line to see the last place runners come in, often several minutes behind the leaders. Yet the runners finishing last could have poured their hearts into the race more so than the winners and done their very best with each step. Cross-country runners do not win ribbons for giving their all. After one demanding run, Jessica told us that over the entire course she had been singing in her mind, "All the Way My Saviour Leads Me." That is both the *how* and the *why* of running our race as God's children and His servants. We have stood at the finish line many times and, because we sense Jessica has done her very best, we have always been able to say "Good race, honey!"

Think of the surpassing joy awaiting each of us at the finish line when by His grace alone we will hear "Well done, thou good and faithful servant" (Matt. 25:21).

A Word in Season

Chapter Four

A Word to Shepherds

"He chose David also his servant, and took him from the sheepfolds: From following the ewes great with young he brought him to feed Jacob his people, and Israel his inheritance. So he fed them according to the integrity of his heart; and guided them by the skilfulness of his hands" (Ps. 78:70-72).

A shepherd is someone who tends sheep, who guides and guards them with watchfulness and patience. God moved David from being a shepherd of four-legged sheep to being a shepherd of two-legged sheep. There is such similarity in both responsibilities that David was well-prepared to make the switch.

Leading by Following

A shepherd is, of course, responsible to lead his sheep, but notice how David positioned himself in order to lead: He was *following* the ewes. How can we possibly lead by following? Picture for a moment General Sherman in the days of the Civil War. Sitting astride his magnificent horse, He turns in the saddle and with a forward sweep of his arm, he yells out in ringing voice, "Forward, men!" This is not how a shepherd leads sheep. They simply will not thunder after the shepherd to do battle with the foe. The best vantage point for a shepherd is behind his flock. However, to move around to the back of the flock with a bullwhip in hand is certainly not the answer either! Sheep would perish under the sting of the lash. It is not the physical position of following that is important to us as spiritual leaders, but the heart position we take that is implied in "following the ewes." These ewes were great with young and needed constant observation. It was for this reason that David got behind them, where he could see them and tend to individual needs. As spiritual leaders, we must position ourselves to be aware of the spiritual, emotional, and physical needs of people. Then we can gently guide in the right direction and not lose sheep to exhaustion or overtaxing. We might believe that people should complete our training course, be placed on the field, and then simply function with minimal problems. We don't think we can afford the time and effort it takes to shepherd them, but we must change our thinking in this. Ewes great with young place constant demands upon our lives as shepherds, but remember that there is also the potential and promise of new birth! If we don't care for missionaries great with potential for God's glory, we lose not only them but the fruit of their ministry as well.

Mixing Patience and Vision

Leaders often have difficulty bringing patience and vision together. We must look ahead with eyes of faith to see the possibilities of advancement; yet, we must also learn how to wait upon God to move in the hearts of those we lead. In fleshly drive and determination, we may force our sheep toward lush pasture only to leave many exhausted and faltering, along the way. We might say, "These sheep just don't have commitment; they are always lagging behind! Send us sheep who can keep pace and cope with the rough ground and hungry lions! We can't afford to waste time waiting for them to catch up or going back to protect them from danger!" Remember that David was accountable to God; he cared for God's people and God's inheritance. We are missing a great truth if we see people only as missionaries with our Mission or as families who attend our local church. The greater truth is that we are *His* people and *His* inheritance and each individual is precious to Him. The application of Psalm 78 is very pertinent and is emphasized in the New Testament; in 1 Peter 5:2-3 we are called God's flock and God's heritage.

Feeding With Integrity

One of David's responsibilities was to feed the sheep, and this he did "according to the integrity of his heart." He always looked for good grass that made wholesome food and healthy sheep. We must not offer the weeds and thistles of human wisdom; only the Word of God is suitable to strengthen the weak. We may have to face up to our slowness and negligence in feeding the sheep constantly. Do we groan as we hear of that missionary who is discouraged again? Or of those two who just can't seem to get along? Didn't we just talk to them? In frustration we might stop feeding and resort to scolding and condemning them for lagging behind spiritually. Not all sheep lag behind. Some bound ahead and are hard to keep sight of! They are always getting themselves and others into dangerous situations. They also need to be fed. As shepherds, we must feed with patience, not only those who lag but also those whose heels we just saw disappearing over the rise ahead. First Peter 5:2 reminds us to feed the flock willingly, not grudgingly. Is there integrity in our feeding, sincerity and honesty in our motivation? Do we truly love the sheep and is our ministry to them without self-seeking? We are not to handle the Word of God deceitfully. We should never seek our own gain or profit. As a good shepherd, David would certainly inconvenience himself in order to bring his sheep to the high pasture with lush grass. We must be willing to expend ourselves if we would feed with integrity. It may mean that, as leaders, we need to place ourselves in a vulnerable position, from which we can be easily misunderstood or hurt because of the ministry of the Word we need to give. It was because the apostle Paul spoke the truth of the Word of God that he felt the pain of hostility from those Galatians who previously had shown great affection for him. He wrote these stirring words to them in Galatians 4:16 — "Am I therefore become your enemy, because I tell you the truth?" We may wonder at this — how truth can make an enemy out of one who has been warned of danger by it. Yet, because the truth disrupts man's spiritual complacency, it is often unwanted, and the one who brings it is treated with coldness and hostility. Are we willing to feed with integrity?

Guiding With Skillful Hands

Not only did David feed his sheep, but guided them skillfully as well. This speaks of drawing upon God as a resource of strength, discernment, and wisdom. David knew well his sheep and their individual characteristics. He probably could tell how each would respond to certain conditions and situations. He made himself familiar with the land and

A Word to Shepherds

the potential dangers. David gave himself wholeheartedly to being a shepherd. It was not a sideline but his life's work. David's skill did not come from natural ability; his testimony is that of one who learned to rely upon God for everything he needed. God had made him skillful. It was God who appointed David as the shepherd of Israel. He certainly would not have chosen him for this task and then expected him to become a skilled leader of people without His help. As leaders, we should not be distracted by our own strengths and weaknesses, ambitions and aspirations. We must be taken up with God, who He is and what He desires. God can make us skillful as we spend time with people where they are, earning their confidence by our love and acceptance of them, listening to them share their fears and frustrations, and helping them make necessary transitions and adjustments.

Knowing that his skill came from God worked humility in David's heart. Many problems could be avoided if we simply learn to listen to those we lead. Let us never be so foolish as to think God will not use His sheep to instruct the hearts of His shepherds. At times, an alert sheep might sense danger where a shepherd expects none, or an observant sheep might smell water that is urgently needed by flock and shepherd alike.

May God help us to be skilled and patient shepherds and also hungry and cooperative sheep!

Chapter Five

DEALING WITH HURT

> "For we know that the whole creation
> groaneth and travaileth in pain together
> until now" (Rom. 8:22).

What a hurting world we live in! Sin's curse lies upon all the earth, and hurt and pain touch every part of creation. Groaning and travailing in pain precedes a birth that is glorious to contemplate — the redemption of our body. But how are we dealing with hurt and pain in our lives *now*, as we wait for this wonderful event? One thing is certain: We cannot go through life without getting hurt! But hurts can be healed, though the healing process itself is often painful. Many people live in constant fear of being hurt and habitually avoid situations or relationships that might cause pain. However, many things are worth doing even though there is the strong possibility of being hurt! I know someone who has been hurt many times playing soccer but still chooses to play. Damaged fingers and toes, a broken nose, a broken rib, surgery on a leg muscle, and numerous bumps and bruises have not convinced him to stop. He is convinced that it is worth the risk to play a game he enjoys! There are, of course, much more important issues in life than a game of soccer. In our involvement with people we often stop short of truly giving ourselves because we are afraid that if we cross some invisible line, we will run the risk of hurt. Intimacy, openness, self-exposure terrify us because we sense our vulnerability and remember hurts sustained in the past. If we are convinced that hurts can be healed, and if we learn how to deal with our hurts, then we can live in liberty and freedom instead of limping along in a spiritually and emotionally crippled state.

The Danger of Storing Our Hurts Away

Our hurts are extremely painful when they first occur, but worse yet, they can be crippling in the years to follow! Because we are generally unprepared to cope with some hurts and there is no one to help us sort them out at the time, we unwittingly store them away in our hearts and minds. Little do we realize what we are doing! When we put money in a bank account, we begin to gather interest so that years later we will have more money than we put in. It is a wise investment. But whoever heard of investing hurt? When we store our hurt away, it too gathers interest, but in the negative sense! Consider some of the "interest" hurt accumulates:

<u>Anger and Rage</u>

There was a crisis in the family of Jacob recorded in Genesis 34 which provides us with a clear illustration of the consequences of not dealing with our hurts. One day Jacob's daughter, Dinah, went to visit some of the young women who lived nearby. She was seen by Shechem, the son of the prince of the Hivites, who took her and had sexual relations with her. When Dinah's brothers heard of this evil deed, we read that they were "grieved" and suffered great distress and pain. We also read that they were "very wroth" or angry (v. 7). We can understand their feelings of pain and anger and we can agree wholeheartedly that what Shechem did was very wrong. However, when Simeon and Levi stored their hurt in their hearts, it festered and grew until it poured forth in vengeful anger and rage. Dinah's brothers tricked the men of Shechem city into being circumcised; then after waiting until they were helpless to defend themselves, Simeon and Levi brutally killed them all with their swords. Years later, when the aged Jacob pronounced the blessings and judgments of God upon his sons, he said, "Simeon and Levi are brethren; instruments of cruelty are in their habitations. ... Cursed be their anger, for it was fierce; and their wrath, for it was cruel" (Gen. 49:5,7).

<u>Bitterness</u>

One of many tragic consequences of not dealing with hurt is that the feelings of resentment we store away are transferable to others. We could call bitterness one of the "communicable diseases" of the heart and mind. Hebrews 12:15 presents this truth very clearly. "Looking diligently lest any man fail of the grace of God; lest any root of bitterness springing up trouble you, and thereby many be defiled."

Because of the unhappy childhood memories of watching parents relate to each other with bitterness, young people sometimes rashly decide that they will never enter into a marriage commitment themselves.

One of the privileges of ministry for older believers in a local church as taught in Titus 2:1-5 is to demonstrate by example what it means to truly love their mates and children and to be free from destructive bitterness in the home. "The aged women likewise, that they be in behaviour as becometh holiness, not false accusers ... teachers of good things; that they may teach the young women to ... love their husbands, to love their children" (v.3-4).

<u>Self-Condemnation</u>

Those who hold onto their hurts often begin to feel that they deserve the hurts they have suffered. This can be understood when we realize that the decision to hold onto our hurts also represents a decision to refuse to acknowledge that God has allowed hurts to touch our lives and in spite of allowing those hurts to bring us pain, He not only loves us, but also places great value on our lives. In Acts 9:15-16, God shows us clearly that when He allows His children to suffer hurt, it is for His Name's sake, that He might be glorified in the life of His child. Speaking to Ananias concerning Paul, the Lord said, "Go thy way: for he is a chosen vessel unto me, to bear my name before the Gentiles, and kings and the children of Israel: for I will show him how great things he must suffer for my name's sake."

<u>Depression, Despair, and Indifference</u>

If we interpret our hurts as an indication of our lack of worth, then we will naturally lose interest in life or in trying to develop a fruitful ministry. Before we can become truly enthusiastic about living, we must be certain of this truth, that God places great value on our lives. Jesus emphasized this truth when He said, "I am come that they might have life, and that they might have it more abundantly" (John 10:10).

The Importance of Depending Upon God for Healing

In our society we are undoubtedly seeing more people with deep emotional hurts than ever before, but we must remember that the answer to our deepest needs is still God. It was God who said, "I will restore to you the years that the locust hath eaten" (Joel 2:25). The coming of locusts into a land meant devastation and loss of productivity for years, so this is God's way of saying that He can work healing and productivity in our lives, even when there has been waste and devastation. But sometimes we do not come to Him for help until we have suffered much and tried many other promising remedies for our hurt but with only temporary help at best. We are something like the woman of Luke 8:43-48,

"And a woman having an issue of blood twelve years, which had spent all her living upon physicians, neither could be healed of any, came behind him, and touched the border of his garment: and immediately her issue of blood stanched."

Christ is the same today as then; He can still work miracles in our lives, healing the deep emotional wounds that cripple and frustrate us. I am not belittling the need for good counsel by spiritual individuals, nor that time is always a factor in our spiritual maturity. The real question is, Where are we looking for our healing? Upon what or whom are we relying? A nineteenth-century songwriter, J. McGranahan, deftly expressed this in "None But Christ Can Satisfy!" The third verse is especially appropriate:

"I tried the broken cisterns, Lord, but ah! The waters failed! E'en as I stooped to drink they'd fled, and mocked me as I wailed. Now none but Christ can satisfy, none other name for me; There's love, and life, and lasting joy, Lord Jesus, found in thee."

Facing Our Hurts and Their Effect Upon Us

The prodigal son had to "come to himself" before he would go to his father for help (see Luke 15:17). His pain became so great he was truly desperate. Fortunately, he humbled himself and reached out for help. Many do not and consequently have a sorrowful end.

Hurts are painful to receive and are often painful to treat. This is why we avoid or put off doing anything about them. We hope they will just go away, but they don't. Small children come to their parents with hurts requiring attention. It hurts them when they get the cut or bruise, but they are usually concerned about the treatment hurting as well! Cleansing their wounds and applying ointment often seem to bring as many tears as actually getting the injury. My mother always used iodine on my cuts, and I dreaded the sting required to ensure proper healing. One day when I was a boy I stepped on a long rusty nail. It went through my sneaker and into my foot, and when I took off my sock I could see where the nail had penetrated my skin. Of course, that meant I needed my first tetanus shot, which I did not look forward to. If I had not faced my hurt, it could have turned out more serious for me. Everyone knows you can't neglect wounds like that. It is just as foolish to try and ignore the emotional and mental hurts we have sustained.

Others in the body of Christ can often help us. As we open up to someone that we trust, we can face how we have been hurt and the crippling effect that hurt has had upon our lives. When speaking with the woman at the well (John 4:16-18), Jesus said to her, "Go, call thy husband, and come hither." With that, He gently exposed an area of hurt in her life, which in this case, also exposed a life of sin. As is often the case, this poor woman had multiplied the hurts she had sustained from others with hurts she inflicted upon herself by her own choices. She liked to think of herself as not having any husband, but Jesus helped her to face the whole sordid mess by saying, "Thou hast well said, I have no husband: For thou hast had five husbands; and he whom thou now hast is not thy husband." In listening to someone sharing their hurts, it is important not to communicate shock or rejection, but instead help them face the hurt with its implications of fear and mistrust. It is obvious that this poor woman was not rejected by the Lord; in fact, she felt so warmed and filled with hope that she went back to the city to bring other hurting people to Him (see vv. 28-29).

Part of the difficulty in facing our hurts is that we must also uncover accumulated attitudes of bitterness, resentment, and even hatred. As Christians we know we should not harbor such attitudes, so we wrongly try to conceal or cover them up. We simply refuse to look at them or admit we have them! God's way for us to deal with these attitudes is to confess them to Him (see 1 John 1:9). An integral part of confessing sin is to face it, which also involves facing the hurts that prompted our wrong choices in the first place.

The Healing Quality of Forgiveness

Where there is hurt, there is a need for forgiveness. Humanistic thought has provided many avenues for people to deal with their hurts. Actually, many of these avenues are really dead-end streets that don't really take us anywhere. A very natural way to deal with hurt is to *hurt back*. Taking revenge is very satisfying in its plotting and execution, but the consequences for the one seeking to hurt back is devastating in the long run. We have no right to hurt one who has hurt us or to take revenge. Romans 12:19 makes this very clear: "Dearly beloved, avenge not yourselves, but rather give place unto wrath: for it is written, Vengeance is mine; I will repay, saith the Lord."

Unfortunately, taking revenge is a greater part of our lives than we perhaps care to realize. Each time we withhold forgiveness from someone, we are choosing to seek revenge or a way to hurt that person

Dealing With Hurt

for what he or she did to us. At times we might lash out verbally or even physically; however, we often try to hurt others by hurting ourselves. Children sometimes seek to hurt parents who have abused or neglected them by involving themselves in crime or immorality.

Forgiving others who have hurt us becomes a very important part in God's work of bringing healing to our lives. If we say, "I will never forgive them for what they did!" then we are still at a point of seeking revenge, and there is no hope of healing for our own hurts. God's Word is clear on this matter: "Let all bitterness, and wrath, and anger, and clamour, and evil speaking, be put away from you, with all malice: And be ye kind one to another, tenderhearted, forgiving one another, even as God for Christ's sake hath forgiven you" (Eph. 4:31-32).

Perhaps it is not entirely a matter of forgiving others for hurting us. We may also need to accept God's forgiveness for how we have hurt Him, others, and ourselves by our own foolish and sinful behavior. We might think God would not wish to forgive us and work healing in our lives because of what we have been or done. However, this is certainly not the case. Nehemiah said, "Thou art a God ready to pardon" (Neh. 9:17). Isaiah said, "He will abundantly pardon" (Isa. 55:7). Christ bore the extreme agony of the cross for us, not Himself. When He cried out at Gethsemane, "Abba, Father, all things are possible unto thee; take away this cup from me: nevertheless not what I will, but what thou wilt" (Mark 14:36). He was looking into a cup filled with our hurts and griefs. All our sins — past, present, and future — were in that cup. He has already taken it up and drained it for us! Isaiah 53:4 puts it beautifully: "Surely he hath borne our griefs, and carried our sorrows." *He longs to assure us of His forgiveness and His commitment to our healing and growth*. Jesus said in John 10:10, "I am come that they might have life, and that they might have it more abundantly." God is interested in the quality of your life. Christians who live with guilt and condemnation are not enjoying abundant life but come far short of entering into what Christ has accomplished for us by His death and resurrection.

Walking in Obedience to God

There is no system of works that we can impose upon ourselves so that we might deserve, earn, or maintain God's forgiveness and favor. Christ has already settled the issue of our salvation once and for all. We stand in His righteousness and are even now accepted before Him (see Eph. 1:6). However, after we have faced our hurts and have sought forgiveness, we must seek to make the choices God indicates are His will for us. As painful memories return, we may again be tempted to turn toward bitterness. We might also be tempted to condemn ourselves and carry guilt because of past failures and sins.

When the religious leaders brought the woman who had been caught in the very act of adultery to Jesus, they thought they had forced the Lord into contradicting Moses' Law, knowing that He would show mercy to her (John 8:1-11). However, His simple statement, "He that is without sin among you, let him first cast a stone at her" set their consciences to work; they all left except the woman herself, who was indeed guilty and knew it full well. She, however, had faced her sin and was now seeking forgiveness and healing. Jesus asked her, "Hath no man condemned thee?" She replied, "No man, Lord." Jesus then said, "...Neither do I condemn thee: go, and sin no more" (vv. 10-11). His forgiveness was freely given, and His counsel was clearly stated: "Go, and sin no more." The scars of mental and emotional hurt that this poor woman bore can only be imagined. Think of the bitterness and resentment she must have harbored in her heart toward men who would treat her so cruelly. Think of the rejection she endured from others and her self — a "no-good," a failure, and an outcast. Then she was forgiven. However, Jesus gave her a very simple direction to follow from that time forward: "Go, and sin no more."

Of all the counselors that ever lived, certainly here was the greatest! Would we have made our counsel to her that simple? For her to please God and grow in her relationship to God, it was necessary for her to choose to do His will and not continue in the way she had been going. *We cannot remain in our old patterns of thought and behavior.* His words to the woman are good for us also, "Go, and sin no more." We develop wrong habits and cultivate wrong attitudes that become quite firmly entrenched in our lives. We might even be blind to them. However, God has committed Himself to our healing, and He has promised that His Holy Spirit "will guide [us] into all truth" (John 16:13). We can trust Him to continue to show us areas of need in our lives; in turn, we must cultivate a mind-set to obey Him.

As you read this you may be conscious of how deep hurts in the past have greatly affected your life in a negative or crippling way. Christ invites you, even pleads with you, to come to Him; He wants to apply to your hurts all that He has already accomplished for you at Calvary.

"Come unto me, all ye that labour and are heavy laden, and I will give you rest. Take my yoke upon you, and learn of me; for I am meek and lowly in heart: and ye shall find rest unto your souls. For my yoke is easy, and my burden is light" (Matt. 11:28-30).

Chapter Six

A CALL TO FAITHFULNESS

> "Therefore, my beloved brethern, be ye stedfast, unmoveable, always abounding in the work of the Lord, forasmuch as ye know that your labour is not in vain in the Lord" (1 Cor. 15:58).

Steadfast, loyal, conscientious, true, committed. These are only a few words that help us define faithfulness. Faithfulness produces both blessing and suffering. We all like blessing but tend to avoid suffering. Yet we cannot have one without the other. Proverbs 28:20 says, "A faithful man shall abound with blessings." Abraham, who was blessed by God, was in turn made a blessing to the world. Nehemiah 9:8 says of him that his heart was found faithful before God. We must also remember that Abraham endured considerable suffering and self-sacrifice. Faithfulness can be costly for us, as in the case of Antipas in the church of Pergamos, whom God called "my faithful martyr" (Rev. 2:13). However, can any suffering in being faithful be compared to the anticipated joy of hearing your Lord say to you, "Well done, thou good and faithful servant" (Matt. 25:21)? Consider the following five questions, and allow the Word of God to minister to your own life.

What Does God Really Expect of Us?

"For if there be first a willing mind, it is accepted according to that a man hath, and not according to that he hath not" (2 Cor. 8:12).

God expects us to be faithful according to what we have to give. He does not expect us to give more than we have to give, even though what we have to give doesn't seem like very much. Remember the five thousand people Jesus fed with only five loaves and two small fishes? Philip spoke for many of us when he said, "but what are they among so many?" (John 6:9). There is so much to do and we have so little to give! What good is it to do even the little we *can* do? What good will it do for us to be faithful? The passage even emphasizes that the two fish were small, yet, as Christ broke them into pieces, about five thousand hungry mouths were satisfied. Don't ask me how He did it — it was a miracle!

If only we are willing, as the verse says, God will accept what we have; in His hands it will be multiplied. When we foolishly look around and see others who seem to have much more talent and ability to offer for service, we begin to compare what little we have with the lot they have, and discouragement soon sets in. Some may have two small fishes to place in His hands, and others may have two full baskets of fishes to place at His feet, but neither are sufficient to feed the crowd without His touch. Remember, He is the one who accepted the two mites of the poor widow and pronounced to His disciples the amazing news that what she had given far surpassed the wealth tossed into the treasury by the rich, whose pockets still bulged as they walked away from the temple (see Mark 12:41-44). She wasn't rich, but she was faithful. She didn't give much, but she gave all that she had.

How Do We Regard Ourselves?

"Let a man so account of us [regard us], as of the ministers of Christ, and stewards of the mysteries of God. Moreover it is required in stewards, that a man be found faithful" (1 Cor. 4:1-2).

Do we regard ourselves as missionaries, teachers, or administrators, or as having certain skills or abilities? It may be fine for us to recognize our own job descriptions, but more than anything else, we ought to regard ourselves as servants of Christ, as those whose chief ambition is faithfulness to Him. Faithfulness is really a motive of the heart. It is what motivates a man to do what he should, when he should, regardless of what people think of him. Actually, it matters very little what others think of you and me. Paul said, "with me it is a very small thing that I should be judged of you, or of man's judgment" (v. 3). Just because others think we are doing a great job does not necessarily mean we are being faithful to our stewardship. What really matters is what God thinks. To please Him, it is absolutely necessary that we are faithful. There are many learned skills that are truly important in our work and so appreciated in our team approach to missionary work. Some are skilled in highly technical areas, helping the work progress more rapidly. Others are gifted in teaching, or administration, to name just a few gifts.

We have certainly become more sophisticated and prepared in our approach to Christian service. What

Moses could have done with a computer to keep accurate tabulations of the thousands of people God had entrusted to Him! Can you think of Paul and Silas traveling on their missionary journeys with their chronological teaching notes in hand? What about John on the Isle of Patmos with a video camera? All kidding aside, thank God for every advancement to speed the spread of God's Word. However, let us remind ourselves constantly that none of these excellent advancements can replace the desperate need we have to be faithful. Only faithfulness is required, because only through faithfulness can God use our lives to accomplish His will.

Is Our Conduct Free of Corruption and Negligence?

"Then the presidents and princes sought to find occasion against Daniel concerning the kingdom; but they could find none occasion nor fault; forasmuch as he was faithful, neither was there any error or fault found in him" (Dan. 6:4).

One translation says,

"They could find no corruption in him, because he was trustworthy and neither corrupt nor negligent" (NIV).

Many people who have served in governmental affairs as Daniel did fall prey to corruption and negligence. Have you noticed how quickly political parties expose any failure in the lives and conduct of those in opposition? We have also seen how quickly and gladly people expose the corruption that is all too prevalent today in the lives of those in Christian leadership. Daniel's life is fresh air to those of us gasping for breath in the smog and pollution of unfaithfulness all around us.

How glad these wicked men would have been to

find some tarnish on Daniel's character, some proof that he took advantage of his position, some record that he directed government funds to his own pocket, some foolish, morally compromising behavior. Yet their search proved fruitless! Would our lives bear such scrutiny? Paul wrote to Titus, "A bishop must be blameless, as the steward of God" (Titus 1:7). Do you long to have a life that is free of corruption and negligence? There is no shortcut to realizing this. To conduct ourselves as good stewards, we must choose to be faithful a moment at a time. If we fail, God's grace is there for us. The father ran to embrace his prodigal son even though his son had wasted all his inheritance in blatant unfaithfulness. Corruption and negligence seem to enter our lives by the small choices we begin to make and then continue to make: entertaining thoughts we shouldn't, putting off doing things that we should do, ceasing to read and meditate daily on God's Word, and "letting things slip" spiritually.

Have We Put the Cart Before the Horse?

"He that is faithful in that which is least is faithful also in much: and he that is unjust in the least is unjust also in much" (Luke 16:10).

Of course, a horse is meant to pull the cart; the cart is not capable of pulling the horse. It makes no more sense to put responsibility in ministry before faithfulness in character. Some feel that as their responsibility becomes greater they will naturally respond with greater faithfulness; however, the cart of responsibility has been placed before the horse of faithfulness. The unfaithful person scoffs at little tasks as though they are too insignificant to bother with. He deceives himself into thinking, *If only I were given something important to do, I could show people how faithful I am! Poor me, I can't be faithful because I don't have anything really impressive to do!*

A faithful person does not stumble over his or her task by trying to evaluate its importance. Instead, that person is concerned with whom he has to please, and no duty is too great or too small. Faithfulness is not determined by the task at hand. Faithfulness is an attitude of the heart that we can choose for ourselves and then apply to each new day and its challenges.

What do you have to do just now? Is there a teaching lesson to prepare or grass to mow? Perhaps you were on your way to see some government official about important matters. Or maybe the drain pipe is clogged up and you need to clean it out. Some tasks throb with excitement while others are quite mundane.

As we learn to choose faithfulness, we understand how to apply ourselves to everything we do with all of our heart. "And whatsoever ye do, do it heartily, as to the Lord, and not unto men" (Col. 3:23).

Are We Reproducing Faithfulness?

"Help, Lord; for the godly man ceaseth; for the faithful fail from among the children of men" (Ps. 12:1).

Science records that in past generations many creatures became extinct due to adverse conditions and failure to reproduce their own kind. Even now many creatures are considered endangered species; they are on their way out unless their fate can somehow be reversed by careful management. What about faithful men and women in the service of Christ? Are they an endangered species? Should we be concerned as the writer of this psalm seemed to be? It appears that throughout past generations, parents have not taught children the importance of faithful attitudes and behavior to the degree that their forefathers taught them. We have lost much of our conscientiousness and commitment to the extent that Psalm 12 definitely seems to be a prayer we should raise to God. What is the use of all the training we receive, the skills we learn, or the tools we acquire if we fail to learn faithfulness? Do we really think we can get the job done without it, or that we can please Him without it? May God give us a longing to learn faithfulness and the ability to instill it in others.

Chapter Seven

A VESSEL UNTO HONOUR

> "If a man therefore purge himself from
> these, he shall be a vessel unto honour,
> sanctified, and meet for the master's use,
> and prepared unto every good work"
> (2 Tim. 2:21).

At some time each of us has picked up a cup or a spoon we needed, but finding it dirty or unwashed, had to lay it aside and select a clean one. A surgeon would not use an unsterilized scalpel to make a crucial incision. If you needed an injection or transfusion, you would want the nurse or doctor to select a clean needle, free from the defilement of some serious virus. As believers, we are like the cup or spoon, and the surgeon's knife or needle. We must be clean spiritually if we would be used by God to serve Him and minister to others in need. Isaiah 52:11 says, "Be ye clean, that bear the vessels of the Lord." The surgeon's knife may have been skillfully manufactured and sharpened to a keen edge, but it is unusable if it is dirty. Many Christian workers have had excellent training and preparation; however, it is not training that qualifies people to be used by God. God can use any vessel so long as it is clean; God cannot use the best prepared vessel if it is dirty.

Is Anything Hidden in Your Tent?

Our attitude toward cleanliness is very important. Many people of the world become sick because they do not understand what germs are, or how disease and sickness are transmitted. Others become sick not because they lack understanding but because they are careless and think, "It won't happen to me, or I can do this just once and it won't make me sick." Are we sensitive to the contaminating effects of sin, and are we careful to keep our hearts pure? We grimace when we see children put dirt in their mouths; do we grimace at a bad attitude in our hearts? We are warned in Hebrews 12:15 not to allow any "root of bitterness" to take hold in our hearts where it can spread defilement, not only in ourselves but also in many others. In Romans 12:9, we are told to "abhor that which is evil." The word *abhor* means to "shudder" with repulsiveness. In Jude 23 we are told to "[hate] even the garment spotted by the flesh." This is said in the context of bringing the gospel to those controlled by sinful lusts. Sadly, missionaries do become enticed by sin because they do not have God's attitude of hatred toward it. An example of this is the sad account of Achan in Joshua 7:21 who took to his heart and his tent some of the spoil belonging to those God wanted completely destroyed. Achan told Joshua, "When I saw among the spoils a goodly Babylonish garment ... I coveted [it]...and took... and hid [it] in the earth in the midst of my tent." Achan found something attractive in that which was spotted (or contaminated) by wickedness. What about us? Do we, like Achan, fight God's battles but find something attractive about the ENEMY? Do we have some "Babylonish garment" hidden in our tent? The ENEMY may not have prevented us from getting into the battle, but we must remember that being in the battle is a dangerous place to be! Obedience to our Commander is essential.

Does Dirt Still Look Dirty to You?

Did you ever notice how you can grow accustomed to a mess on your desk or to dirt in the corner, so that you are not bothered by it as you once were? As time passes, we can accept clutter and dirt as part of our surroundings and no longer work toward picking up and cleaning up. This is how we are spiritually also. If we begin to tolerate any degree of spiritual filth, we are also beginning to accept its presence in our lives. Sin can look like a viable option to a person who is blinded by it. No wonder the Word of God in at least four New Testament references, encourages us to "flee" from sin: "flee fornication," "flee from idolatry," "flee also youthful lusts," "flee these things [foolish and hurtful lusts, and love of money]" (1 Cor. 6:18; 10:14; 2 Tim. 2:22; 1 Tim. 6:11). It is significant that our English word *fugitive* comes from the word *flee* as used in these references. A fugitive is one who is running away or seeking to escape. We might not always be able to flee the actual physical surroundings as Joseph did (see Gen. 39:12), but we can flee from sin by a simple choice to obey God's Word.

Our Wonderful Uncompromising God

We really serve a wonderful and gracious God. He is holy and hates sin, yet He loves us as sinners and has provided a way in Jesus Christ for us to be saved from sin's penalty and from sin's *power*. God does not compromise with evil. He never sits down at some bargaining table to dialogue with evil in an attempt to reach a settlement. God reached His own settlement regarding sin on the cross where our Lord suffered and died — there is nothing more to talk about! Habakkuk 1:13 says of Him, "Thou art of purer eyes than to behold evil, and canst not look on iniquity." Jesus echoed the meaning of Habakkuk's words when He cried out, "My God, my God, why hast thou forsaken me?" (Mark 15:34). Christ bore the awful filth of our sin upon His own sinlessness. He took the anguish of sin's consequences in our place; He broke forever sin's power to control our lives. Shall we choose to permit sin an entrance into our hearts, or tolerate its intrusion upon the fellowship we have with a loving and holy God?

Are You Clean and Usable?

Perhaps your heart aches because you realize that all is not what it should be in your life. Attitudes toward co-workers, bitterness regarding your circumstances, and sinful desires of the flesh all represent uncleanness and spiritual uselessness. Be reminded and encouraged, God has made provision for you to be cleansed! The promise recorded in 1 John 1:9 has certainly been claimed billions of times by saints down through the centuries, but it is as trustworthy today as when it was first written by the apostle John. "If we confess our sins, he is faithful and just to forgive us our sins, and to cleanse us from all unrighteousness." Don't turn away as the unclean leper Naaman once did on the banks of the Jordan (see 2 Kings 5), but plunge unhesitatingly into His ocean of forgiveness and cleansing.

Chapter Eight

ARE YOU SUCCESSFUL?

"The desire accomplished is sweet to the soul" (Proverbs 13:19).

Most of us have a difficult time considering ourselves successful and often as we look back over our days, months, and years, we are dissatisfied with what we have accomplished. I guess it must be because of the way we evaluate success in our society and culture. Money is a big factor. So is the matter of having a large following or being popular or in demand. Success might mean having done what we think others expect us to do or what we have expected of ourselves. We all evaluate our lives, especially as we realize we have set our course and precious time is passing. For some, this is a time of panic because there is an awareness of not having gained money, recognition, or popularity, or not having done what we think is expected of us.

As I thought about my own life, I realized there

have been both failures and accomplishments, but I was really filled with joy as I realized that God's definition of success does not depend upon whether I have accomplished some personal goal that exalts or promotes me in some way.

We are all prone to seek our own success, but that only proves to be an empty search.

The rich farmer of Luke 12 was extremely successful by his society's standards. His land produced to the point where he had to contemplate building bigger barns to hold his produce, yet God called him a fool because all his accomplishments were only for himself. God also in this passage gives us a look at what true success is in the phrase "rich toward God" (Luke 12:21).

Because of talents, opportunities, personality, finances, or other things, we might appear to be successful, yet our lives only bring glory to ourselves. The only true success is to glorify God. Success to me is living so as to please my God and bring glory to Him. This is not accomplished primarily by external things (for example, how much I do) but by the condition of my heart. Is His glory and pleasure really the goal, priority, and objective of my life? Jesus said, "My meat is to do the will of him that sent me, and to finish his work" (John 4:34).

When I awake each morning to start a new day, is it my work I set about to do, or is it His? If it is my will and my work, then I will undoubtedly struggle with attitudes of jealousy and competition toward those with whom I am supposed to do His work. If success to us is to please Him, then our course is set, and we make daily choices and decisions accordingly.

These moment-by-moment choices to live to please Him and allow Him to glorify Himself through our lives and circumstances keep us from the disaster of being sidetracked. Paul, as he came to the end of his life said, "I have finished my course" (2 Tim. 4:7). This emphasizes to me that Paul did not get sidetracked but kept on the course God had set out for him, not because he realized great personal achievement and accomplishment but because it was what God wanted, and that was enough. Don't we often compare ourselves to others and what they are doing and soon become dissatisfied and feel like failures? When Peter saw John, he could not help but compare himself with that disciple who seemed to have a special earthly relationship with the Lord, so Peter said what I have often thought concerning others I know or work with: " Lord, and what shall this man do?" Jesus, always tender and gracious yet firm in His guiding of His own, replied, "...what is that to thee? follow thou me" (John 21:21-22). In my own heart, I can sense an emphasis on His words, "follow thou me." Truly, that is enough, and it is success as the world cannot know! Maybe it does not seem as though we are doing much, especially in comparison to someone else, but success cannot be measured in how much we are doing. God has a wonderful way of multiplying.

It is not how much we do but whether we do it out of a desire to please Him whom we love. True success is seldom noticed; in fact, it is often missed altogether because we do not see as God sees. I find I must continually choose to be content with myself and serve Him out of love with the gifts He has given me.

Sometimes in our determination to be a success for God, we strive in our own strength like Jacob. Jacob tried very hard to succeed, but the harder he tried, the harder his way became. We still strive this way at times, even though we know better. Our fleshly determination to succeed and be something for God is strong in us, but it is counterproductive to true success. Hebrews 11:6 says, "Without faith it is impossible to please him" (God), which makes clear to us that faith in God is essential to success. As we place our confidence in God and walk obediently in His way, He succeeds in bringing glory to Himself through our lives.

Consider this humorous illustration of the counterproductivity of striving in our flesh to succeed in pleasing God.

Suppose for a moment that you were called to the home of an elderly friend because her cat had climbed a tree and could not get down. Desiring to be very helpful, you went immediately to her house, climbed the tree and having retrieved the cat, delivered it safe and sound to your delighted friend. As you saw your friend's genuine gratitude and watched her cat playing happily in the yard, your heart swelled with satisfaction that you had succeeded in doing a good deed and making your friend very happy. Getting in your car you cheerfully waved good-bye, backed up to leave, and ran over the cat.

How many times I have "run over the cat" in my fleshly determination to succeed in pleasing God. I'm sure it adds up to a lot of cats but mercifully, God is gracious and very patient.

Chapter Nine

REMEMBER TO ENCOURAGE

> "Wait on the Lord: be of good courage,
> and he shall strengthen thine heart: wait,
> I say, on the Lord" (Ps. 27:14).

This verse is a clear definition of what it means to be encouraged, to be inspired with courage and to have our hearts strengthened! It also shows us that the only true source of encouragement is the Lord Jesus Christ, and if we would encourage others, we must direct their attention to Him.

It Costs to Neglect Encouragement

We need to encourage one another as much as we can. It seems that the ENEMY is doing all he can to weight us down with problems and difficulties. We all get so busy in our particular aspect of the work that we often neglect to give one another encouragement. Often when we have difficulties in our work relationships, the last thing we think of doing is simply encouraging. Encouragement is tragically low on our list of priorities when thinking of heading out to the tribes. If we constantly encouraged each other, we would not have the problems we do.

Refreshed by Encouragement

How sensitive we should be to the cares and burdens of those we work with! Jesus, in love for His disciples said, "Let not your heart be troubled" (see John 14:1). Another time, He lovingly washed their dusty, tired feet and then reminded us that we should look for ways to refresh one another (see John 13:15). Very often we need to be refreshed with a reminder that no matter what difficulties we face or what failures we have had, nothing can prevent God from loving us. Paul encouraged the Roman Christians with that truth when He wrote Romans 8 and exclaimed that nothing could separate us from the love of God. There is not one of us who does not desperately need encouragement. If, in our particular location, we can encourage those we work with, the entire "family" can be strengthened.

Love and Acceptance

The greatest way to encourage others is to assure them that we love and accept them completely. We all do our work much better if we know we are loved and appreciated, even though we may fail. Our failures and shortcomings seem to loom large, and the ENEMY quickly uses our wrong focus on these things to further discourage us. What a blessing it is for our co-workers to simply communicate love and understanding to us at that point! Encouragement can make the difference between someone staying in ministry or succumbing to discouragement and quitting.

Jonathan the Encourager

How often David must have been discouraged when King Saul relentlessly chased him and was determined to kill him. How much David must have longed to know he was loved and that someone was standing with him. In 1 Samuel 23:16 the account is given of Jonathan, Saul's son, seeking David out simply to encourage him. "And Jonathan Saul's son arose, and went to David into the wood, and strengthened his hand in God." If only we could strengthen our co-worker's hand in God! How tragic if we should weaken his hand in God instead! One thing that enabled Jonathan to care so for David and strengthen him was that Jonathan was not at all jealous of or in competition with David. Jonathan knew he would be "next" to David or under him, but he did not care. Jonathan loved God and David also, and that love prompted him to encourage David. Without love we only criticize, find fault, disagree, become negative, or remain silent while our co-worker is hurting because of problems or failures.

The Tender Encouragement of God

How tender, loving, and encouraging is our heavenly Father, even when He sees our weakness and frailties. Isaiah 42:3 says, "A bruised reed shall he not break, and the smoking flax shall he not quench." We can so carelessly say a crushing word or indicate our disapproval and even feel righteous in doing it. But when God sees we are "dimly burning" (smoking flax), He does not blow us out contemptuously but nourishes and encourages us. Do you remember how He did this with Elijah when that prophet was so discouraged and filled with self-pity? Elijah, exhausted after having fled from Jezebel, fell asleep murmuring that he wanted to die — that it was no use, he was no good, he was not appreciated, no one was standing with him, that he had served God faithfully for nothing, and that he felt very much alone. I wonder what I would have done had I come across Elijah right at that point? I might have reprimanded him for his unbelief and pointed out his self-pity! How gently God treated his discouraged prophet! He sent an angel twice to touch him and invite him to eat. As a result of this encouragement, Elijah arose to serve God and disciple his successor, Elisha.

The Hard-Line Approach

How readily we take the hard-line approach with others but desire the "soft-line" approach for ourselves. We must always be honest but never have an attitude of giving up on each other or coming down hard on others. The latter only serves to discourage and crush what is already weakened. None of us like to be treated roughly; instead, we crave tenderness and gentleness. How much easier it seems to respond to tenderness than to roughness! Our enemies — the world, the flesh, and the devil — are all rough on us and by no means encouraging. In view of this, how much more vital it is for us to seek every opportunity to sow love and appreciation.

The Encouragement of Lovingkindness

David spoke of the "lovingkindness" of God and we realize this was a tremendous encouragement to him throughout his life. During the darkest times David prayed, "Shew thy marvellous lovingkindness" (Ps. 17:7); "Remember, O Lord, thy tender mercies and thy lovingkindnesses" (Ps. 25:6). David kept himself from discouragement by focusing his attention on the lovingkindness of God and said, "Thy lovingkindness is before mine eyes" (Ps. 26:3). David recognized that we have a great responsibility to encourage others in the way that God has encouraged us. David wrote, "...I have not concealed thy lovingkindness ... from the great congregation" (Ps. 40:10). This is borne out in the New Testament in 2 Corinthians 1:3-4, where Paul explained that one very important reason God encourages us is so that we can encourage each other. He wrote, "Blessed be God, even the Father of our Lord Jesus Christ, the Father of mercies, and the God of all comfort; who comforteth us in all our tribulation, that we may be able to comfort them which are in any trouble, by the comfort wherewith we ourselves are comforted of God." How wrong it is for us to come down hard on others in our attitudes and words when God has come down so kindly and gently upon us!

The prayer of David in Psalm 40:11-12 could so easily be the prayer of any believer. David saw countless difficulties on all sides; wherever he turned he ran into trouble and seeming impossibilities. He also saw his own sins, so he became depressed and weighted down. How many of us have been, or are, this despondent? Oh, for a word of encouragement at such a time! David found his encouragement in the lovingkindness of God and confessed that without it, he would surely have "quit and gone home." Notice how David writes all this: "Withhold not thou thy tender mercies from me, O Lord: let thy loving kindness and thy truth continually preserve me. For innumerable evils have compassed me about: mine iniquities have taken hold upon me, so that I am not able to look up; they are more than the hairs of mine head: therefore my heart faileth me "(Ps. 40:11-12).

Encouragement or Irritant?

We can help preserve one another by the comfort of our love, the "love of God shed abroad in our hearts" (see Rom. 5:5). Even Paul faced trouble on the outside and fears on the inside, and at a crucial time in his life when he was facing discouragement, along came Titus, sent of God especially to encourage Paul and his company. "For, when we were come into Macedonia, our flesh had no rest, but we were troubled on every side; without were fightings, within were fears. Nevertheless God, that comforteth those that are cast down, comforted us by the coming of Titus" (2 Cor. 7:5-6). What Jonathan was to David, Titus was to Paul. Is there a David or a Paul we can seek out simply to encourage? We need only look to those in our families, in our local church, or serving with us in ministry. This undoubtedly, is the greatest thing we can do as part of the body of Christ — to encourage and comfort. Paul said of Onesimus, Aristarchus, Marcus, and Justus, "These only are my fellowworkers unto the kingdom of God, which have been a comfort unto me" (Col. 4:9-11). The word *comfort* means "soothing" and was used to refer to medicines that remove irritations. We sometimes speak humorously of being used by God as sandpaper to smooth off the rough edges of others. But our desire should be just the opposite; that is, not to irritate one another, but to encourage and comfort. The three co-workers of Paul were not an irritant but an encouragement.

Conclusion

We are always excited when new people come into our fellowship or join our particular work, and we immediately evaluate what they can do to help out. Perhaps they can fix broken tools and equipment.

Perhaps they have linguistic abilities that promise to speed up language learning.

We can contribute to our work in many ways, but the greatest, most long-lasting contribution we can possibly make is the encouragement we give to others.

Chapter Ten

OUR SPIRITUAL PERSPECTIVE

> "Not unto us, O Lord, not unto us, but
> unto thy name give glory, for thy mercy,
> and for thy truth's sake" (Ps. 115:1).

There are many personal possessions that we may not wish to lose, but we could live very nicely without them. However, if we lose our spiritual perspective, the consequences spell disaster. Our spiritual perspective is our view of the absolute importance of seeking God's glory and believing God's Word. The only alternative is to seek our own glory and to trust in our own wisdom. The one who seeks God's glory and believes God's Word is God-centered, while the one who seeks his own glory and trusts in his own wisdom is self-centered.

Paul, when writing to the Philippian believers, expressed his desire to send Timothy to them. Paul knew that Timothy was God-centered and that he would seek God's glory, looking to God for wisdom when he was among these believers. Paul also expressed his sadness over the fact that there was a serious shortage of men who had this spiritual perspective. He wrote, "For all seek their own, not the things which are Jesus Christ's" (Phil. 2:21).

It is possible for God's servants to lose their spiritual perspective and to flounder spiritually in self-centeredness.

Such a man was Elijah. The Bible tells us that "Elias was a man subject to like passions as we are" (James 5:17), so we can readily identify with him in becoming discouraged; but we can also learn with him as God faithfully ministers to his life to restore his spiritual perspective.

Victorious on the Mount

There he stood. Against him were eight hundred fifty evil prophets, and wavering in unbelief in the background were the multitudes of silent onlookers, intent upon the seemingly uneven contest, eager to know what the outcome might be. His bold challenge rings out from the top of Mount Carmel, "How long halt ye between two opinions? if the Lord be God, follow Him: but if Baal, then follow him" (1 Kings 18:21). Listen to him again as he mocks these foolish, wicked men who are leaping and cutting themselves in a frenzy. "Cry aloud" he mocks, "... either he is talking, or he is pursuing, or he is in a journey, or peradventure he sleepeth, and must be awaked" (v. 27).

Elijah watches all day until the prophets of Baal fall in exhaustion and frustration. Now it is his turn, and in confidence he commands that the sacrifice be soaked with twelve barrels of water before he prays that God will make Himself known and turn the hearts of Israel to Himself. Fire from the Lord fell to consume sacrifice, wood, stones, dust, and water, and all the people fell on their faces to acknowledge, "The Lord, He is the God" (v. 39).

Even yet the prophet is not finished: "Take the prophets of Baal; let not one of them escape" (v. 40), he shouts, and bringing them down from the mountain, Elijah put to death those evil men who for so long had deceived and intimidated the people. Certainly this is enough for any man for one day! But no, warning Ahab to ride fast to Jezreel in order to get there before the rain stopped him, Elijah began running himself, and actually outran the horse and chariot in the fifteen mile run from Carmel to Jezreel.

Defeated Under the Bush

Having read this stirring account of Elijah's victorious confrontation with the wicked prophets of Baal, it is difficult to accept that this is the very same man who now sits defeated and asking to die under a juniper tree in some deserted part of Beersheba.

It began days earlier when a messenger had come to Elijah with this message from Jezebel, "So let the gods do to me, and more also, if I make not thy life as the life of one of them by to morrow about this time" (1 Kings 19:2). In short, Jezebel promised to kill Elijah just as he had killed her false prophets, and this she promised to do within twenty-four hours.

This is not such an unusual story, really. Don't we see the same thing happening today among our own co-workers and God's servants everywhere? How many missionaries have served God faithfully for years — learning a difficult language, bridging tremendous gaps of culture, teaching the truth of the Word of God, shedding light in spiritual darkness, working out difficult problems in relationships with co-workers — and then one day, find that it is all too much to take; the thought of escape seems irresistible, even absolutely necessary! But, for Elijah, escape was not an answer, nor is it for us; it only leads to severe depression and a loss of the will to live and serve God.

Spiritual Problems Have Spiritual Answers

Elijah certainly had gone through some high-stress situations and demanding physical exertions! Certainly we know from the record given in 1 Kings 19:5-8 that when God's angel woke him, there was food and water prepared for his nourishment and strengthening. Elijah went for forty days and forty nights on the strength of that meat. However, the problem was not one of physical exhaustion but of losing spiritual perspective; for Elijah was still running away, even after God had fortified him with nourishment. It certainly helped to have the rest and the food, but that did not solve Elijah's *spiritual* problem.

When we are weary and tired physically and emotionally, it is important to get away and find rest — perhaps a change or diversion; but when we are discouraged and fearful, we face a spiritual problem that cannot find a solution apart from a spiritual work of God in our hearts. We may escape from the physical location of our problems and devote our energies to a pursuit of rest and relaxation; however, if we do not face our spiritual need we might simply be like Elijah, still running and still desperate (see vv. 8-10).

Are You God-Centered or Self-Centered?

When we are spiritually down, we may not even want to be refreshed! Elijah tried to find seclusion in a cave (see 1 Kings 19:9). We might try to escape in other ways, but if we should find ourselves home from the mission field and discouraged, we may not want to be disturbed by the attempts of others to encourage us.

Although Elijah certainly had been under stress, his real heart problem was that he had lost his spiritual perspective. Once he had looked in faith to almighty God and found grace for every situation. Now he sought to find strength to face life's trials from his own inner resources, and he came up empty. Once he desired only that God be glorified, and that desire motivated him to face the problems at hand and see God work them out. Now he was afraid for himself, and his concern was self-centered. This is by no means a criticism of Elijah but an observation of what caused him to seek to remove himself from the very situation that only days before brought glory to God.

In many cases (not all), this is our problem when we decide to give up, to quit, to resign, to stay home, or to seek a change of ministry. Compare these two heart expressions of Elijah to see the difference in his perspective. The first is on the mount: "...let it be known this day that thou art God in Israel, and that I am thy servant." The second is under the bush: "...*I* have been very jealous for the Lord God of hosts ... and *I*, even I only, am left; and they seek *my* life, to take it away (1 Kings 18:36; 19:10, italics added). It is not difficult to see which of these perspectives is God-centered and which is self-centered.

Elijah's spiritual perspective or viewpoint on Mount Carmel had been God's glory; however, when Jezebel's servant delivered her evil message to Elijah, the prophet made a crucial choice to trust in his own strength and take care of himself

There Is Nothing Discouraging in God

We may be able to gain the pity or sympathy of others when we are discouraged, but it doesn't change the fact that self-centeredness is sin and is a spiritual problem.

We cannot solve a spiritual problem by physical means. If we are resentful and bitter toward our spouse or co-worker, it is self-centered seeking of our own glory, and we cannot gain a right attitude by a good night's sleep or a one-year furlough. If we are discouraged because of personal failure, inadequacy, or weakness, it is a self-centered concern, and we cannot encourage ourselves by proving that we are strong, adequate, and successful.

Elijah was as weak and inadequate in himself when he stood boldly against eight hundred fifty prophets as when he sat, miserable and despondent, under the juniper. The difference was a simple choice and change in the attitude of his heart. Elijah's spiritual perspective had changed from God-centeredness to Elijah-centeredness.

Whenever I have wanted to run or have entertained thoughts of quitting, it has always been because of self-centeredness. There is nothing discouraging in God, and it is impossible to be God-centered and indulge in self-pity. When the angel awoke Elijah, he said something very significant. He said, "Arise and eat; because the journey is too great for thee" (1 Kings 19:7). The angel was reminding him that his wild self-centered plunge was taking him away from the true source of all strength and comfort.

The End of Yourself

Elijah's flight took him to Horeb, the mount of God, where the angel of God had appeared to Moses in a flame of fire out of the midst of a bush (see Ex. 3:2) and where Moses wrestled with his own self-centered inadequacy. Moses had, like Elijah, run away from one who threatened his life, and his flight had taken him to this desert place. Moses offered many excuses why he could not return to face his adversaries in Egypt, but God showed him that he needed the right spiritual perspective. He needed to have a God-centered heart.

We could think of Mount Horeb as "the place of coming to the end of yourself." It was also in this range of mountains that God gave to Moses the Ten Commandments, which showed clearly, the utter impossibility of pleasing God in the energy of the flesh. This was indeed a fitting location for Elijah to find himself.

How graciously God seeks to restore His spiritual perspective. God never lifts us out of our spiritual doldrums by having us stare at ourselves in the mirror. He always intends to show Himself to us. He wants you and me to be God-centered men and women. Finding Elijah in the self-centered seclusion of the cave, He said, "Go out and stand on the mountain in the presence of the Lord, for the Lord is about to pass by" (1 Kings 19:11, NIV). After the strong wind, the earthquake, and the fire passed by the cave's mouth, Elijah heard God's voice as a gentle whisper and, wrapping his face in his mantle, he went outside to humbly stand before God.

How often after we see our sin of self-centeredness we expect the wind, earthquake, and fire of God's anger and rejection. But how wrong to expect this of the God who has said, "There is therefore now no condemnation to them that are in Christ Jesus" (Rom. 8:1). Our lives are often like the sea spoken of in Psalm 107:27-29, "They reel to and fro ... and are at their wits' end. Then they cry unto the Lord in their trouble, and he bringeth them out of their distresses. He maketh the storm a calm, so that the waves thereof are still."

Go Back the Way You Came!

It is not God's will that we run away from trials or problems. He wants us to return in faith to where we lost our spiritual perspective. God said to Elijah, " Go back the way you came" (1 Kings 19:15, NIV).

God still had plans to glorify Himself through His prophet, and those plans could not be fulfilled in a mountain cave in Horeb. In our self-centeredness, we leave a lot of work undone; we leave a lot of people still unreached; we leave a lot of relationship problems still unsolved.

Why Does Everything Seem So Negative?

When we lose our spiritual perspective of God-centeredness, we also lose our spiritual perspective of what God is doing. All seems dismal, and we cannot seem to think of anything positive about where we are working or the people we are working with. It is not uncommon for discouraged missionaries to speak only negatively and pessimistically about their tribal station or the field headquarters where they work. To them, no one seems to be walking with the Lord, needs are not being met, nobody is getting along, and no one understands them.

Elijah was in this state when he said to God, "I, even I only, am left" (1 Kings 19:10). When God restored Elijah's spiritual perspective, He also helped the prophet to look realistically upon what He was doing in Israel. God said to Elijah, "Yet I have left me seven thousand in Israel, all the knees which have not bowed unto Baal, and every mouth which hath not kissed him" (v. 18).

God Has Plans for You

God certainly did continue to glorify Himself through Elijah's life; in fact, Elijah went out of the cave in Hebron a changed man. His spiritual perspective was again God-centered, and it showed in his life. Wicked Ahab trembled before him and said,

"Hast thou found me, O mine enemy?" (1 Kings 21:20). Concerning Jezebel, who once sent him fleeing for his life, Elijah said, "The dogs shall eat Jezebel by the wall of Jezreel" (v. 23).

God can do for you what He did for Elijah. If you realize you are spiritually self-centered, stand in the presence of God and allow Him to restore your spiritual perspective. God still has definite plans for your life that can become reality only if your heart is centered on glorifying Him.

Chapter Eleven

WHAT IS YOUR DUTY STATUS?

"No man that warreth entangleth himself with the affairs of this life; that he may please him who hath chosen him to be a soldier" (2 Tim. 2:4).

The armed forces have definite procedures for keeping track of personnel during wartime. Each day roll call is taken; if personnel answer to the call, they are classified as *reporting for duty*. If they do not answer, they are classified as *duty status whereabouts unknown*. No longer than ten days are permitted to elapse before personnel in this category must be reclassified into such categories as *missing in action*, *killed in action*, or prisoner of war *POW*. Of course, they can be located and returned to the status of *reporting for duty*, which is the ideal outcome.

In the spiritual warfare in which we are presently involved, we can apply these categories in a general way to our Christian lives and service to God.

A Report on Personnel

Joseph was *reporting for duty*, as seen by his response, "Here am I" (Gen. 37:13). When his father asked him to search for his brothers, Joseph was gone like a hound on the trail. It was as though Joseph had no other plans or ambitions but to do his father's will. If only that were our heart attitude constantly! Another man, of whom Joseph was merely a type, expressed his heart in this way: "My meat is to do the will of him that sent me, and to finish his work" (John 4:34). The disciples wanted Jesus to take some food for His body's sake but to Him, doing His Father's will was nourishment and gave purpose to life. What is nourishment to you? What gives purpose to your life? A soldier does not report for duty with a schedule of his own. He does not write his own orders. He simply presents himself as available to carry out the orders of his commanding officer. Sometimes I think of this in the morning, at the start of a new day. If I am not careful to quiet my heart before God and take time to wait upon Him, I find that I simply lunge like a racehorse at the starting gate, eager to start the day's contest on my own.

Jonah and Elijah had to be classified *whereabouts unknown* (of course, God knew where they were). God found Jonah trying to escape his assignment by ship, and He located Elijah under a bush, frightened and very depressed. Both were missing in action for a time but reported for duty again after God worked in their lives. How the classification *duty status whereabouts unknown* makes me think of my own life! Saved as a boy, I became discouraged by ridicule in high school and distracted by the ways of the world. Consequently, I stopped following the Lord in obedience. Like Jonah, I took to a ship — only for me it was the Navy. I still remember one fierce storm that tossed the waves one night and beat against our big ship. I'm very glad I was not tossed overboard to be swallowed by something lurking in the depths below! Those were indeed unhappy days for me, as all time spent out of fellowship with God must be.

Can I testify to the loving graciousness of the Lord in bringing me to my senses and giving my heart the desire to report for duty? I lost valuable time that could have been spent living for Him, but I love Him for dealing patiently and truly with me, and I never want to be missing in action again.

Stephen was *killed in action*, as were many others. They were faithful unto death (see Acts 7:54-60; Heb. 11:36-38). God asks us that by His grace, we remain "faithful unto death" (Rev. 2:10) which to the Christian and because of the work of Christ, is not a defeat (see 1 Cor. 15:54-57).

Sampson failed to report for duty one day after visiting Delilah and later was found a *POW* of the Philistines. They were to regret taking him prisoner, however, for we read in Judges 16:30, "So the dead which he slew at his death were more than they which he slew in his life."

A POW Reporting for Duty?

It is possible and probable for soldiers to report for duty outwardly but not inwardly. That is, they may simply stand at attention at roll call and gain the classification *reporting for duty*, but in their hearts they might not want to serve their country and may even grumble at the orders given them. However, for Christians it is a vastly different matter. God looks on our hearts and is not deceived by our mere presence at "roll call." We could be working at our jobs as missionaries but be classified spiritually as a *POW* because our hearts are not right with God. We can go about our daily tasks like a piece of well-oiled machinery but without heart. Our work and ministry may have the appearance of success because the machinery is working smoothly. However, if sin is in our lives and we are living in the energy of the flesh, we are merely spiritual *POWs* and our labors are fruitless. Jesus spoke these words:

"Abide in me, and I in you. As the branch cannot bear fruit of itself, except it abide in the vine; no more can ye, except ye abide in me" (John 15:4).

A Prisoner by Choice

Of course, becoming a *POW* in the battles of this world is a very real risk that a soldier must accept. If disarmed or disabled by the enemy, a soldier has little or no choice. His fate is determined strictly by his captors. However, such is not the case with a Christian and his spiritual battle. Because of the victorious and finished work of Christ on the cross, no Christian can become a spiritual *POW* outside of his own will. Our spiritual ENEMY simply does not have the power or authority to bring us under bondage. "Knowing this, that our old man is crucified with him, that the body of sin might be destroyed, [to render idle, inactive, inoperative] that henceforth we should not serve sin. Let not sin therefore reign in your mortal body, that ye should obey it in the lusts thereof. For sin shall not have dominion over you" (Rom. 6:6,12,14). We may not feel like making the right choice in times of temptation to discouragement, anger, and ungodly thinking, but our feelings cannot be relied upon to direct us in God's way. We must choose contrary to our feelings and decide upon the course God has set for us in His Word. As Christians, we are free not only from the penalty of sin but also from its power; tragically, we do not always claim that freedom but instead allow sinful attitudes and actions to dominate us daily. Mr. L.E. Maxwell, in his book *Born Crucified*, writes of the soldier who reported to his commanding officer, "I have taken a prisoner." His commander said, "Bring him along with you." "He won't come," complained the soldier. "Well, then, come yourself," replied the officer. "I can't. He won't let me," was the final acknowledgment.

This is exactly how sin controls our lives and prevents us from reporting for duty.

The Battle and the Victory Is the Lord's

We do not want to strain this analogy by making too much of a comparison, but as believers in this hostile world we are in a battle more real, vicious, and intense than the one recently played out in the Middle East. It is important that we remain on the alert and in the category *reporting for duty* until He takes us home to be with Him.

Concerning some of the wars fought on this earth, it is possible that there were no real winners; however, one thing is very certain: we *are* on the winning side in our spiritual battle, and even now the victory unquestionably belongs to the Lord of Lords and King of Kings. May we serve Him faithfully!

Chapter Twelve

CONFLICT!

> "For, brethren, ye have been called unto liberty; only use not liberty for an occasion to the flesh, but by love serve one another... But if ye bite and devour one another, take heed that ye be not consumed one of another" (Gal. 5:13,15).

Paul's description of the flesh in conflict is one of savagery and viciousness! The words *bite* and *devour* were commonly used by the Greeks to describe the fighting and attacking of wild bloodthirsty animals as they fought for mastery over, and often the death of, their opponent. One animal would inevitably be consumed by the other; it is what is sometimes called the law of the jungle. Paul uses this picture metaphorically to suggest a likeness between the nature of the beast and the nature of the flesh.

As we compare verses 13 and 15, we see the clear choice believers have. We may serve one another by our love for each other, or we may consume one another by our biting and snapping. Of course, the flesh is never motivated by love, and it cannot serve anyone but itself. The Holy Spirit, on the other hand, who was sent by Christ to comfort and enable us, would never consume or destroy what is so precious to God. He would only prompt and enable us to serve each other. Conflict is born of the flesh, but we do not have to walk in the flesh; we have the simple divine solution to walk in the Spirit (or under His control), and we will not fulfill the lusts or desires of the flesh to bite and devour whoever gets in our way.

When I was teaching on the subject of "conflict among missionaries," one of the students related an excellent illustration of the biting, devouring, consuming nature of the flesh. He told of working with pigs and how the boars often would become enraged at the sight of another male competitor. Even though in a different pen, one boar lunged at the boards separating him from the object of his rage until he managed by brute force to partially break through the boards in a vicious effort to inflict damage on the other boar. In so doing, he snapped off one of his own tusks and in succeeding days suffered much pain because of it. When we walk in the flesh, we are like this enraged boar. We are being controlled by the lusting of the flesh and are bent on expressing our hostility, unaware of the mental and emotional pain sure to follow, uncaring of the spiritual damage and devastation that we cause ourselves and others.

The Blessings of Differing Viewpoints

It is unavoidable that we have opposing or differing viewpoints about many things. In fact, it is healthy that we do. Here are three blessings resulting from our relationship with co-workers or other believers with differing viewpoints:

Differing viewpoints increase our effectiveness in ministry. Proverbs 27:17 says, "Iron sharpeneth iron; so a man sharpeneth the countenance of his friend." Two pieces of iron rubbing together can sharpen each other. As two missionaries work through disagreements under the Spirit's control, they also can have this effect on each other. As a team we can, in this same way, increase our effectiveness in completing the job which God has given us to do. Because we have always done something a certain way does not mean that is the way we should continue to do it. When another missionary has a different idea than ours, we often feel threatened and personally attacked. We may dig in our heels refusing to budge or react in the flesh some other way, but the ensuing conflict will prove to be negative and counterproductive to our ministry.

Differing viewpoints aid us in evaluating our own lives. We should always value the insights of others, especially observations that lead us to a healthy and constructive evaluation of our habits and attitudes. Perhaps the differing viewpoints of our co-workers may reveal the need for change. We should not react in the flesh by becoming defensive, resentful, and hostile when our ideas or opinions are disagreed with. Proverbs 18:15 says, "The heart of the prudent getteth knowledge; and the ear of the wise seeketh knowledge." The wise believer referred to in this verse is always open to new ideas; in fact, he looks for them!

Differing viewpoints assist us in knowing the mind of the Lord. There is not a man or woman among us who does not need counsel or advice. Proverbs 23:12 says, "Apply thine heart unto instruction, and thine ears to the words of knowledge." One paraphrase of this verse is, "Don't refuse to accept criticism; get all the help you can." Do we really want to know the mind of the Lord, or are we more interested in promoting our own ideas and opinions? We may feel so strongly about something that we are not at all open to hearing another's opinion; the flesh reacts in resistance and antagonism toward others. How easy to forget that we wage a spiritual battle with an ENEMY skilled at deception. We must heed Proverbs 24:6, "For by wise counsel thou shalt make thy war: and in multitude of counsellors there is safety."

On What Shall We Blame Conflicts?

It is certainly possible to work through differing viewpoints without conflict. Our goal should always be to find the mind of the Lord. God wants us to find likemindedness. Paul wrote, "Fulfil ye my joy, that ye be likeminded, having the same love, being of one accord, of one mind" (Phil. 2:2). To be likeminded is to think the same thing or to have harmony in our thinking. This is impossible if fleshly pride is controlling our lives. If we are experiencing conflict with another believer and it seems impossible to resolve, it would be a mistake to blame it on personalities or incompatibility. The real problem is in our hearts, and it is simply pride. Proverbs 13:10 says, "Only by pride cometh contention." Can we not simply believe what God says and agree with His assessment of our problem? Humanistic thought is forever offering alternatives to God's simple assessments and solutions to our spiritual problems. What humanistic psychology offers to us seems so much more respectable and easy to take than God's simple statement, "He that is of a proud heart stirreth up strife" (Prov. 28:25). There are many proud arrogant people today who are being advised by counselors that they need to get in touch with the violence within them (whatever that means). What we really need to do is to humble our hearts before God and of course, before one another. Proverbs 22:10 says, "Cast out the scorner, and contention shall go out; yea, strife and reproach shall cease."

Consequences of Conflict

The consequences of conflict are much too devastating for us to allow it to continue. Here are three consequences that we must take a hard look at:

1. When we are in conflict with another, we magnify his or her faults and weaknesses.

It is easy to find areas needing continued growth in another person's life that we can point to in an attempt to discredit him and promote ourselves. Galatians 5:15 warns us that in our biting and devouring of another, we will end up consuming him. The word *consume* means "to destroy or waste." All of us need much encouragement, and we have the privilege of giving this to one another. This would have the effect of supporting and giving strength. The ENEMY is seeking to do just the opposite and, sadly, we often play right into his hands by taking away the supports of encouragement, leaving our fellow believer used and spent. We can only speculate how many of God's servants decide to leave their place of ministry because of unresolved conflict with believers.

2. Conflict causes division.

Division may occur within the family, the team, the local church, or a mission organization. In Mark 3:24-25 Jesus gave us a very clear principle concerning the results of division: "And if a kingdom be divided against itself, that kingdom cannot stand. And if a house be divided against itself, that house cannot stand." The worst attack on a house or kingdom comes not from outside but from within. Often we actually grow stronger, more unified, and committed to our task when attacked by enemies of the gospel from without, but we can easily crumble when eroded by division from within our ranks. Proverbs 6:16,19 tells us of God's displeasure toward the one "that soweth discord among brethren."

3. When we are in conflict, we expend our energies on nonproductive activities.

Our fleshly attitudes of resentment, jealousy, and competition drain us of physical, mental, emotional, and spiritual strength. We cannot concentrate during our work times or really rest at our leisure times. We become preoccupied, not with productive things, but with hashing and rehashing situations of conflict. Walking in the flesh, we become like wild beasts who might be found either lapping their own wounds or plotting ways to inflict injuries on others. We wear ourselves out physically and emotionally by being contentious and antagonistic. King Saul foolishly wasted all his time and energies chasing David instead of the Philistines, who eventually took his life. It was a simple tune sung by the women of Israel that caused Saul to become enraged by his jealousy over David's successes (see 1 Sam. 18:7). From that time forward, Saul lost any true leadership perspective he might have had and became obsessed with his fleshly fear that David would get his job and position.

God's Priority for Our Relationships

Our priority in our relationships should be to glorify God together, and to serve Him together in the oneness He has already accomplished. Ephesians 4:3 calls us to live out this priority:

"Endeavouring to keep the unity of the Spirit in the bond of peace." "Endeavouring" speaks of doing one's best, of making concentrated effort to "keep" or guard with care the oneness and agreement that is already in our possession and is a product of the Holy Spirit. How foolish to disregard such a treasure, such a bond of peace! Paul pleaded with the Corinthians, "Now I beseech you, brethren, by the name of our Lord Jesus Christ, that ye all speak the same thing, and that there be no divisions among you; but that ye be perfectly joined together in the same mind and in the same judgment" (1 Cor. 1:10).

Chapter Thirteen

SPIRITUAL REALITY

> "Joash was seven years old when he began to reign, and he reigned forty years in Jerusalem.... And Joash did that which was right in the sight of the Lord all the days of Jehoiada the priest.... But Jehoiada waxed old, and was full of days when he died;... Now after the death of Jehoiada came the princes of Judah, and made obeisance to the king. Then the king hearkened unto them and they left the house of the Lord God of their fathers, and served groves and idols"
> (2 Chron. 24:1-2,15,17-18).

The story of Joash is a very unusual one. When he was born, the political scene in Judah was filled with conspiracy and intrigue. His wicked father had been violently killed (see 2 Chron. 22:9), and his own grandmother was intent upon destroying all possible descendants to the throne, even her own grandchildren, so great was her lust for power (v. 10)! Because of this, Joash was hidden when he was only one year old and remained in concealment the next six years of his life (v. 12). With such an uncertain start, we might hold out little hope for Joash to do well in life; however, God had tremendous opportunities in store for this young boy in the form of a God-fearing priest named Jehoiada. This courageous leader led the people in putting down the wicked reign of Joash's grandmother, Athaliah, and restored the throne to its rightful young king, Joash (see 23:3).

Joash stepped up to the throne when he was only seven years old, but God had given him the example and teaching of Jehoiada to guide him during those tender formative years and work spiritual reality into his life. It appears, however, that Joash did right only because of the strong influence of Jehoiada, for when this godly priest died, Joash was easily led into idolatry by the princes of Judah. When God, in mercy, sent Jehoiada's son Zechariah to warn him of divine judgment upon his sin, Joash killed him in cold blood (see 24:22). Joash revealed little evidence of God having worked in his life through the many years of Jehoiada's influence. He did not even show appreciation for the memory of Jehoiada himself; he killed his benefactor's godly son, simply because he dared challenge his idolatrous practices.

Opportunities Are Not Enough

If anything should convince us that the benefits of godly example, sound teaching, and all of God's gracious opportunities are not equivalent to spiritual reality, the account of Joash should! Joash looked like a godly man while Jehoiada lived, but when that priest died at one hundred thirty years of age, the real Joash appeared, no doubt to the utter shock of many in Judah. No wonder God severely cautioned Samuel when that prophet, impressed with Jessie's tall, handsome son, Eliab, was about to anoint him king. God spoke these words that should mark themselves indelibly on our minds: "Look not on his countenance, or on the height of his stature; because I have refused him: for the Lord seeth not as man seeth; for man looketh on the outward appearance, but the Lord looketh on the heart" (1 Sam. 16:7).

The condition of our hearts determines the course of our lives. If God is working in our lives, then when tested and pressured by humanistic thought or by ungodly influences, we will at least have a good basis for choosing right. However, if we are simply living properly because of the strong godly influences of others, then when those influences are lifted, we will surely drift off course and into ungodliness. Joash did what was godly all the days of Jehoiada, but when he was called upon to propel himself under his own steam, he quickly went off the tracks.

Appearances Are Not Enough

Outward appearances — how easily we are deceived by them, both in our own lives and in the lives of others! As God said, this is where we naturally look to see whether what appears on the outside is reality on the inside? Thankfully, God can see within the heart of man, and He has committed Himself to revealing our true spiritual needs to us. Hebrews 4:12 says, "For the word of God is quick, and powerful, and sharper than any twoedged sword, piercing even to the dividing asunder of soul and spirit, and of the joints and marrow, and is a discerner [critic] of the thoughts and intents of the heart." This was the very reason Christ promised to send the Holy Spirit. Jesus said, "Howbeit when he, the Spirit of truth, is come, he will guide you into all truth" (John 16:13). The Holy Spirit of God, using the Word of God, faithfully tells us the truth about ourselves.

We do not need to fear being deceived if we are dependent upon God and obedient to Him; however, if our confidence is in our own human wisdom, we will surely be deceived by our pride and exalted opinions of ourselves. Did He not caution us, "Trust in the Lord with all thine heart; and lean not unto thine own understanding. In all thy ways acknowledge him, and he shall direct thy paths" (Prov. 3:5)?

God was not able to reach and teach the heart of Joash, even though He had provided for Joash a godly teacher and example. Joash certainly did not lack knowledge of who God is and what He is like; perhaps he was deceived by his pride.

Knowledge Is Not Enough

Interestingly enough, although knowledge is necessary for reality in our hearts, it is also the cause of conformity or mere outward appearance. We are sometimes deceived by the fact that we know so much. Gaining knowledge is a necessary step to faith and spiritual reality as Romans 10:14 evidences: "How shall they believe in him of whom they have not heard?" But knowledge also can incite us to pride and arrogance: "Knowledge puffeth up" (1 Cor. 8:1).

God gives knowledge that man might act upon that knowledge by believing and obeying Him; but if we just accumulate more and more knowledge, we become proud of all we know and begin to think that *what* we know is the same as *who we are*. However, knowledge is not equivalent to reality. We can accumulate a lot of knowledge, but we cannot turn what we know into spiritual reality; only God can do that in response to our faith and obedience.

Our pride is a much greater hindrance to His working than our lack of knowledge. Humility of heart, on the other hand, is the fertile ground necessary for God to work reality in our lives. James 1:21-22 admonishes us to "receive with *meekness* the engrafted word" and to "be...doers of the word, and not hearers only, deceiving your own selves" (italics added). Without a meek, submissive spirit, we become knowledge-gatherers only. We might be able to parrot back all we know and even do so in an illustrative way, but it is without reality or without God's work being done in our hearts.

Right Performance Is Not Enough

Sometimes we see an extreme change of attitude and action in the lives of those who sat under sound teaching and had good spiritual examples to emulate. Notice the extreme change of doing good and evil in the life of Joash by comparing these two verses:

"And it came to pass after this, that Joash was minded to repair the house of the Lord" (2 Chron. 24:4). "Thus Joash the king remembered not the kindness which Jehoiada his father had done to him, but slew his son" (v. 22).

Joash seemed as easily enthused about destroying God's house as he had been about repairing it! Joash was easily influenced to do good or evil because there was no solid core of reality to hold him firm or give constancy to his life. Unless God has done a work in our hearts, we can change quickly and drastically, depending upon what situations or people are influencing us. The chameleon is easily changed by his surroundings. This slow lizard can change into five different colors and even present a spotted appearance! He changes into green, yellow, white, brown, or black as a result of variations in light or temperature — or even because he is frightened. When Joash "changed his color" and killed Jehoiada's son, it seemed the very height of ingratitude and contempt for what Jehoiada had stood for. When people come into knowledge but do not allow God to turn that knowledge into spiritual reality, they are unknowingly preparing themselves to despise the truth they were taught because they know it clearly stands opposed to what they really want to do.

When God gives us the opportunity for discipling

another, whether it be in the context of raising a family or teaching in a local church, we must never be content just to see right performance. We cannot work in another's heart; only God can do that. Philippians 2:13 says, "For it is God which worketh in you." As vessels of God, we must direct a person's attention and thought to what God says, believing God will apply that truth to their hearts. We should not look with suspicion and doubt on those we disciple, but we should not just assume God has done a spiritual work simply because people say the right things, come regularly to meetings, or display other acceptable Christian behavior.

Getting Excited Is Not Enough

Our modern way of thinking does not encourage God's working in our lives. We love to be entertained all the time, even when being taught spiritual truth. We want to hear dynamic speakers who can hold us spellbound by their skills of oration. We want to listen to singing groups that are exciting. Nothing dull and drab for us! We are in danger of falling into the trap carefully laid for us: "If you want to compete for people's attention in this world, you have to do things professionally." For example, the word is out that slide presentations are no longer the way to go; missionaries should use the more effective means of video to challenge people into missions. Although people can get excited about hearing the dynamic speaker or watching the professionally produced videos, is this going to work a change in their hearts? Or can these "more effective means" of communication actually be a hindrance to what God wants to do in their lives? We should not hesitate to use the best or most effective means of communication God has placed at our disposal. The point is this: Unless God works in a person's life, there can be no reality. There may be an excited, enthused outward appearance, but that will affect people's lives only as long as they are being kept excited by the outside influence, just like Joash who did what was right all the days of Jehoiada, but not after.

Being Persuaded Is Not Enough

The apostle Paul was very much aware of the danger of influencing people only to the point of an outward appearance. In writing to the Corinthians about his visit to them, he said, "And I brethren, when I came to you, came not with excellency of speech or of wisdom, declaring unto you the testimony of God... and my speech and my preaching was not with enticing words of man's wisdom, but in demonstration of the Spirit and of power: that your faith should not stand in the wisdom of men, but in the power of God" (1 Cor. 2:1, 4-5). Paul's ministry among the Corinthians purposely lacked any persuasive pressure of his own. Paul's attitude was one of utter dependence upon God to work spiritual reality in the lives of the Corinthians as they heard a clear and simple presentation of God's testimony.

Our Confidence Must Be in God Alone

This must also be our attitude, both for our own personal lives and also for the lives of those we minister to. Our confidence must be in God alone to work spiritual reality in our hearts as we humbly sense our need of Him. Except for God's working, there can be no spiritual reality.

David said it this way: "Except the Lord build the house, they labour in vain that build it" (Ps. 127:1).

Chapter Fourteen

IN SOMEONE'S THOUGHTS

> "How precious also are thy thoughts unto me, O God! how great is the sum of them! If I should count them, they are more in number than the sand: when I awake, I am still with thee" (Psalms 139:17-18Ps. 139:17-18). "O Lord, how great are thy works! and thy thoughts are very deep"
> (Ps. 92:5).

That "someone" is God. It may be obvious that God thinks about you, but did you ever wonder *how* He thinks about you? From the two psalms above, we can learn at least four lessons pertaining to God's thoughts toward us.

Lesson One:

God's Thoughts Have Loving Intent
"How precious also are thy thoughts unto me, O God!"

Things that are precious are of great value and worth to us. We treasure them and find them very desirable. This is precisely how we should consider God's thoughts toward us and yet, all too often, believers can find their hearts suspicious toward God

In Someone's Thoughts

and even fearing what His thoughts or intentions might be toward them. God has no intent to harm or injure us. In fact, when speaking to His people Israel, whom He had permitted to be taken into miserable slavery, He spoke very significant words revealing His true intent not only to them, but to all who are precious to Him. "For I know the thoughts that I think toward you, saith the Lord, thoughts of peace, and not of evil, to give you an expected end" (Jer. 29:11). We realize from looking at the context and also from comparing other scriptures that God's expectation for us is that our lives might glorify Him. This is what makes God's thoughts toward you and me precious — He always thinks about us in relationship to His glory and because of this, His thoughts are always for our good. Our good cannot be separated from His glory. If something occurs in our lives that is not for His glory, it cannot possibly be for our good, no matter how pleasant and desirable it might seem to us.

Perhaps a favorite question the ENEMY likes to ask us at crucial times of suffering is this one: "If God loves you, why is He allowing this to happen to you?" He might quickly follow his question with a suggestion: "Either God can't control what is happening to you or He doesn't care what is happening to you!" Frankly, it is hard for me to believe that God thinks about *me* at all! I can more easily believe that He thinks about important things like keeping the planets in orbit and patching up the hole in the ozone layer. Actually, I can even believe He thinks about other believers I know, but I sometimes wonder that He could even care that I exist at all. My doubts do not change the fact that God does think about me, but they do reveal my lack of understanding of Him and how intimately He cares for me.

Notice how David emphasizes the intimacy of God's thoughts when He says, *"Thy* thoughts unto *me."*

Knowing what God's Word says, it is up to us to believe it. God really cares about us. That is why Peter wrote to those who were suffering persecution, "Casting all your care upon him; for he careth for you" (1 Pet. 5:7). Some of the greatest pain people feel today is that "nobody really cares." In this world, it's easy to feel like a number. A quick look in my wallet shows me that I am identified to various branches of government and organizations by eight separate numbers! I finished my responsibilities in the navy almost thirty years ago, but I can still rattle off my serial number just like I was standing at attention! When God said, "I care for you," He meant that you are His concern. He doesn't worry about you because God has no need to worry, but He has more interest in your life than you could ever have. God not only cares for us, but He cares with the purpose that our lives bring Him glory. Sometimes on the surface things may look chaotic and confusing, but we must remember that part of what makes God's thoughts precious is the fact that they are purposeful. He has started glorifying Himself in your life and mine, and His thoughts are to bring that purpose to completion. Philippians 1:6 is our reminder: "Being confident of this very thing, that he which hath begun a good work in you will perform it until the day of Jesus Christ." In Romans 8:38-39 Paul writes that nothing can separate us from God's love. In fact, the very things we fear most and have the least control over can never alter the fact that God is "for us" in His thoughts (v. 31). Death, life, angels, principalities, powers, things present, things to come, height, depth, any other creature — they are all listed in this passage. Though we are confronted by all these influences, God is still "for us." When faced with chaotic and confusing events, there are two responses we can have. We can ask, "If God really loves me, why is He allowing this to happen?" Or, we can choose the confident, "Even though this is happening to me, God really loves me!"

Lesson Two:

God Leaves Nothing to Chance in Your Life

"How great is the sum of them! If I should count them, they are more in number than the sand."

When God wanted to impress man with a very great number, He sometimes had him try to count the stars or consider the grains of sand on the ground. If you want to get an idea of how many thoughts God has about you, go to a beach (even a small one) and try to count even a handful of the grains of sand! The point is, you cannot do it, nor can you count high enough to find the total of His precious thoughts toward you. Does that sound incredible? It is, but it is true as David wrote in Psalm 40:5, "Many, O Lord my God, are thy wonderful works which thou hast done, and thy thoughts which are to us-ward: they cannot be reckoned up in order unto thee: if I would declare and speak of them, they are more than can be numbered."

By His numberless thoughts of you, God is emphasizing that no detail of your life is overlooked. Nothing just happens. There is no such thing as a lucky or tough break.

God and chance do not go together. He thinks about every aspect of your life and orders your steps according to His purpose to glorify Himself in you.

Chance is the foundation of evolutionary thought which gives no glory to God as the Creator and Sustainer of all things. In Luke 12:6-7 Jesus expressed how detailed God's thoughts are about His creation. He said, "Are not five sparrows sold for two farthings, and not one of them is forgotten before God? But even the very hairs of your head are all numbered. Fear not therefore: ye are of more value than many sparrows."

There are those who foolishly believe that God created all things but then let them evolve as they would. In other words, God starts things going but then takes His hand away to let them develop however they might. Think of the awful consequences if this were true! We would never know when God had left us and chance had taken over! However, even the sparrows created by God are not forgotten by Him. In fact, even the hairs of your head are kept on account before God just so you will be convinced that God allows nothing to occur by chance without His knowledge and control.

Lesson Three:

God Cannot Be Distracted From Thinking About You
"When I am awake, I am still with thee."
When I was a small boy and extremely ill with a high fever, my mother sat beside my bed at home. Of course it was a comfort to have her tuck me in and try to make me comfortable, but the greatest comfort, and that which has remained as a precious memory, was to find her still with me whenever I awoke in my tossings. She remained with me because I was in her thoughts continually. In much greater measure, God is thinking of us always. To be distracted means to have the focus of attention diverted from something because of the urgent demands of other happenings. It is often accompanied by confusion or bewilderment. I have often thought with amazement how God can care for the universe and all things in it yet not lose one second of thought concerning you and me. He not only created all things, but as Colossians 1:17 tells us, by Him all things "consist" or hold together.

Lamentations 3:22-23 says, "It is of the Lord's mercies that we are not consumed, because his compassions fail not. They are new every morning:

great is thy faithfulness." God's compassionate thoughts toward you and me are unceasing (fail not) and they are fresh and applicable to each new day. Sometimes circumstances and situations in our lives seem to indicate that God has forgotten us, that His gracious thoughts toward us have ceased. Usually, it is because of sorrow we face or persecution that comes to us. David knew much of both and expressed himself in Psalm 13:1-2 this way: "How long wilt thou forget me, O Lord? for ever? how long wilt thou hide thy face from me? How long shall I take counsel in my soul, having sorrow in my heart daily?" However, God never forgets.

In Isaiah 49:15-16 God said, "Can a woman forget her sucking child, that she should not have compassion on the son of her womb? yea, they may forget, yet will I not forget thee. Behold, I have graven thee upon the palms of my hands." God, who thinks about you continuously, cannot forget you for a moment.

This same truth is emphasized in Hebrews 13:5-6 with the thought of God not leaving us. "I will never leave thee, nor forsake thee. So that we may boldly say, The Lord is my helper, and I will not fear what man shall do unto me." When a person forsakes another as an unfaithful husband might forsake his wife, the forsaking begins in the mind and thoughts but inevitably results in actual abandonment. God, however, cannot forsake or abandon us because He never stops thinking loving thoughts about us.

Lesson Four:

God's Thoughts Are Hard to Understand Because They Are Wise
"O Lord, how great are thy works! and thy thoughts are very deep."

The meaning of "deep" is unsearchable and hard to

understand. God's thoughts toward us are sometimes hard for us to understand, not because God's thoughts are confusing, but because we are unable to grasp His wonderful purposes for us.

We do not always think wisely; instead, we often think with only immediate consequences in view. Even when we do attempt to think wisely, ours is only a limited wisdom, unable to see life with the all-wise perspective of God. One holiday we went as a family to the Ontario Science Center. That day the Center had set up an elaborate maze for people to go through. At first we saw it from the perspective of an upper story and could look down upon it. Except for some obstruction, we could see quite clearly the end from the beginning and we felt so much wiser than the people wandering around inside. However, a little later we went through it ourselves, and our perspective was also limited by the walls of the maze and the many choices before us. Life is often like a maze to us, but it is never a maze to God. Psalm 139:12 says, "The darkness and the light are both alike to thee."

This is where we often find our struggles; because we cannot understand what God's thoughts are, we become confused and panicky, thinking things are out of control and in chaos. God helps us to understand our problem by these words in Isaiah 55:8-9: "For my thoughts are not your thoughts, neither are your ways my ways, saith the Lord. For as the heavens are higher than the earth, so are my ways higher than your ways, and my thoughts than your thoughts." His thoughts are described as being "very deep" (Ps. 92:5) and also being very high (see Isa. 55:9), certainly higher than our thoughts! While our thoughts are *limited* by being earthly, His thoughts, *elevated* high above temporal things, are on an entirely different level of wisdom and understanding. God is all-knowing and all-wise. He is not limited at all by lack of knowledge or wisdom as we are.

Paul, in Romans 11:33-34, breaks out into wondering praise to God for the "depth" of His thoughts. "O the depth of the riches both of the wisdom and knowledge of God! how unsearchable are His judgments, and his ways past finding out! For who hath known the mind of the Lord? or who hath been his counsellor?" When Psalm 92:5 says of God "Thy thoughts are very deep," we should compare that with this truth in Romans 11:33 to understand that the depth of God's thoughts are His wisdom and knowledge.

He knows all the implications of the course He has set for our lives. He lacks no knowledge of future events that relate to your life. Kings, prime ministers, and presidents need advisers, but God does not need anyone to advise Him. God, who thinks such loving and purposeful thoughts about you and me, longs that our hearts might also be occupied with Him. David said in Psalm 104:34, "My meditation (thoughts) of him shall be sweet: I will be glad in the Lord."

Chapter Fifteen

STRENGTHEN WHAT REMAINS

> "Be watchful, and strengthen the things which remain" (Rev. 3:2).

These words spoken by the Lord to the church at Sardis have important application to believers, local churches, and Christian organizations.

The Cost — of Neglect

Man does not readily learn by history and continues to repeat his mistakes, bringing disaster to his enterprises. One of our greatest errors is to neglect to maintain what God has enabled us to obtain. We begin to take what we have for granted, not remembering what it took by way of blood, sweat, and tears to build it up.

Proverbs 24:30-34 give us Solomon's observation of this: "I went by the field of the slothful, and by the vineyard of the man void of understanding; and, lo, it was all grown over with thorns, and nettles had covered the face thereof, and the stone wall thereof was broken down."

As Solomon considered what he had seen, he concluded that it was simple neglect that eventually brought ruin to the slothful man. It was not that the man had tried hard to have productive fields and vineyards but had failed because of poor judgment; it was simply that he had done nothing. Slothfulness is not only the neglect of material things; it can also be seen in the neglect of spiritual things, but the end result is the same — poverty.

A man builds a beautiful house with lovely grounds prepared around it. He is good at planning and building but weak in maintaining and upkeep. Soon his house looks shabby and the grounds run-down.

A group of men join together to build a company known for its high standards of quality and production. They know what they want for their company's objectives, and they know how to train their employees to produce the kind of merchandise they want to put on the market. Soon their label is associated with quality, and their product is greatly desired. However, these men are not sensitive to the need to maintain these high standards in the attitudes of their workers, and eventually the company loses its quality control and production drops off.

What is the problem and how does it affect us as believers? It is not enough to build strong training programs and develop effective church planting techniques. It is not enough to enter new countries and place more missionaries in tribal locations. We must also continually be strengthening that which remains of what God has enabled us to build.

The church at Sardis had evidently lost or let go of some spiritual truths that were once dear to them, and their service was adversely affected. The Lord said, "I have not found thy works perfect before God" (Rev.

3:2). It is not physical or material things that we are concerned about primarily, but spiritual things that God has entrusted to us.

The Contrast — Slothfulness And Watchfulness

The contrast of being watchful (Rev. 3:2) and being slothful (Prov. 24:30) is one we must not miss. The slothful man neglects what God has given, while the watchful man is careful to strengthen what remains. Slothfulness or watchfulness — one of these attitudes will characterize us, and the corresponding results will eventually be seen. To be watchful is simply to be on guard and alert and is a command given to believers several times in the New Testament. For example, in 1 Thessalonians 5:6 Paul again contrasts slothfulness and watchfulness with these words: "Therefore *let us not sleep*, as do others; but *let us watch* and be sober (italics added)." The very fact that God has placed this admonition in His Word should alert us to the danger of becoming slack and our need to be on the alert.

That the church in Sardis was once established with a very positive testimony and effective outreach seems evident by these words: "Thou hast a name that thou livest" (Rev. 3:1). How was it that the believers in Sardis had neglected to maintain the work that God had done in their midst? When did they cease being watchful, and why had they taken what God had done for granted, not placing great value on the spiritual truth that had been taught them previously? The change was probably gradual and took place as individuals lost their grip on spiritual truth and ceased encouraging one another to be true and faithful.

The Question — Who Is Responsible?

We may wholeheartedly agree that someone needs to see to the strengthening of the believers in our local church or the missionaries in our mission — but who? We must not for a moment pass this responsibility on! Each of us is equally responsible to see that our mission or church fellowship is strengthened in God, that His will may be done.

Do we know how to strengthen each other spiritually by giving support and assistance? We have been taught much about teamwork and functioning together. Some missionaries are even classified as support personnel; but in reality, are we not all supposed to support one another? Does not the Bible say that we all need one another? Who in the body of Christ can say to another, "I have no need of thee" (1 Cor. 12:21)?

Can you imagine watching your favorite team in the super bowl and seeing the quarterback throw a long arcing pass to a receiver who makes a splendid catch and begins sprinting for a touchdown? The opposition cannot possibly touch him, and the game is as good as won! But what is this?! As you watch with unbelieving eyes you see, not the opposition, but a member of the receiver's own team throw a tackle that sends the receiver sprawling and the ball squirting from his grasp. Something obviously went dreadfully wrong. What the opposition could not do, his own teammate did! Perhaps it is hard to imagine something like that happening, and perhaps it never has; however, did you ever stop to think how we believers are sometimes guilty of tackling our own teammates?

It takes more than a uniform to make an athlete a team player. What we need is a work of God in our hearts, strengthening us in the spiritual truths of loving, accepting, and appreciating one another so that we function as a body.

The Division — Caused by Independence

Fleshly independence causes us to see anyone "with the ball" as the opposition. We must carry the ball ourselves or tackle whoever has it, no matter what the color of his uniform. This is doing things "through strife or vainglory" (Phil. 2:3).

We can only contribute to the strengthening of others if we have no aspirations of our own for glory and praise. In fact, Philippians 2:3-4 says it this way: "In lowliness of mind let each esteem other better than themselves. Look not every man on his own things, but every man also on the things of others."

One of the surest ways the enemy has to weaken our work is to bring division of some kind into our fellowship. Jesus said: "If a house be divided against itself, that house cannot stand" (Mark 3:25). One way division enters any team or work is through the selfishness and independence of its members. Although many details about our ministries may vary because of different settings of culture, etc., we cannot afford to assume the attitude of being independent and each doing our own thing. Of course, this possibility greatly increases as we become larger in number and more spread out in location, but this only increases our need to be spiritually alert and responsive to God.

The Confusion — Caused by Unfaithfulness

How soon we forget to value those simple, fundamental truths that were so life-changing to us in earlier days! The admonition is clear to us: "Remember therefore how thou hast received and heard, and hold fast, and repent" (Rev. 3:3).

The question for each of us to ask ourselves is,

"Are we holding fast to what we received?"

Second Timothy 2:2 is familiar to all of us: "And the things that thou hast heard of me among many witnesses, the same commit thou to faithful men, who shall be able to teach others also."

A faithful man is one who values those things he was taught and strengthens himself in them so he can in turn strengthen others.

One of the greatest causes of confusion in the local church comes as a result of believers not faithfully continuing to walk in the light they have received through the teaching they have been given. The attitude "Do as I say, not as I do," is devastating to discipleship in the local church, the family, and in missionary organizations. Our lives are extremely frustrating to others if our attitudes and our behavior are not consistent with what we claim to believe. This is especially true for us who are in any spiritual leadership. Those watching our lives for an example of how they should live so as to please God should not expect to see perfection, but they should be able to see faithfulness to the Word of God demonstrated in a commitment to walk consistently in its light.

The Commitment — To Strengthen Each Other

If we should see anything concerning the ministry of our local church or our mission organization that needs improvement, we should bring it to each other's attention so that appropriate changes can be made. We cannot afford to let things go and get run-down by neglect; nor can we afford to assume we do not need each other and decide to go our separate ways. Each of us must be watchful to strengthen the things which remain.

Because of the human element in our ministry, there is much that needs strengthening. It is human nature to be critical and faultfinding. It is divine nature to be faithful and gentle, building up that which is weak and feeble. As Christians, we can choose to allow God to live through us and in faithfulness and gentleness, we can be committed to strengthening each other. It was written of the Lord, "A bruised reed shall he not break, and the smoking flax shall he not quench" (Isa. 42:3). Only God can give us this same attitude and enable us to care for each other so that our desire for each other and our fellowship is strengthened to serve and glorify God.

The Solution — Strengthen as We Advance

Strengthening is as important as advancing. Unless he knows the enemy is defeated, a general would be foolish to advance far into enemy territory without seeing to his supply line. If cut off from food, ammunition, and supplies, a mighty army can be reduced to a starving multitude in a very short time.

The last responsibility God gave to His servant Moses was not to perform some great individual effort but to strengthen his successor, Joshua. God said, "But charge Joshua, and encourage him, and strengthen him: for he shall go over before this people, and he shall cause them to inherit the land which thou shalt see" (Deut. 3:28). If Moses had neglected the strengthening of Joshua, the whole operation of Israel conquering the land might well have bogged down.

Of course, we must move forward and continue to advance into new areas of ministry and opportunity, but we must also strengthen ourselves as we do so. In speaking to Israel, God set forth a principle that applies to us: "Enlarge the place of thy tent, and let them stretch forth the curtains of thine habitations: spare not, lengthen thy cords, and *strengthen thy stakes*" (Isa. 54:2, italics added).

Revelation 3:2 implies that if we do not strengthen those things entrusted to us, we will not have them long! Listen to what it says: "...Strengthen the things which remain, that are ready to die."

The Encouragement — As God Has Enabled Us to Build, He Will Enable Us to Strengthen

God never asks us to do what He does not enable us to do. Look around you, and you will see many opportunities to strengthen others; by doing so, you will strengthen the work of the Lord as a whole. As you see other believers "running with the ball," you can run alongside and lend the support and encouragement they need to cross the "goal line." As you remember truths you have received and have been careless with, you can choose to hold them fast, even sharing them afresh with others. As you think of those areas of difference you have had in your heart and mind with other believers, you can seek, by God's help, to find oneness of mind where it is needed.

God has enabled us to advance into many areas of ministry and into many countries of the world with wonderful opportunities to serve Him and make Him known. Let us not forget the need we share individually and collectively to be strengthened in God.

Chapter Sixteen

LISTENING

> "Wherefore, my beloved brethren, let every man be swift to hear, slow to speak, slow to wrath: for the wrath of man worketh not the righteousness of God" (James 1:19-20).

There is a simple device available to you that could greatly assist you in maintaining godly, harmonious relationships. It doesn't cost any money and can be taken with you anywhere and applied to any relationship, whether in your family, among unsaved people, or among other believers. It is the simple ability God has given you to listen to others, and more importantly, to listen to God Himself.

The old Rabbis used to point out that God gave man only one mouth but two ears, and he left the ears open but enclosed the tongue behind a wall of teeth! David said it much better in Psalm 141:3 — "Set a watch, O Lord, before my mouth; keep the door of my lips." How many relationship problems do you know of that are a result of being too quick to listen? On the other hand, how many problems are you aware of that have resulted from a quickness to speak? As we examine the four main parts of these verses in James, we will be challenged afresh to listen to each other.

"Swift to Hear"

Our Objective in Listening

Perhaps our reason for listening stops short of the real motive we should have if we listen to others simply to understand what they are saying or thinking. Although this is important and a good motive in itself, it is not the most important reason for listening. Primarily, our reason for listening to others should be to gain understanding of what God is seeking to communicate and how He would have us respond to Him. According to our verse in James, the reason for listening is that God might have His own way in our relationships.

In the various struggles, small and great, that we experience in our relationships, we should always strive in the Spirit to understand and submit to God's righteous purposes. If this were our intent, there would always be profit in our interaction, and God's work would continually go ahead. However, when we find ourselves needing to work through difficulties with others, we seem to be unconscious of the opportunity to find out what God wants and consequently, wedges are driven between hearts, and God's work through us suffers. True listening can change our entire outlook on how we relate to each other and can open up our understanding of God's purpose in any situation.

Listening Can Be Painful

We all realize that speaking before a group, or even to one person, can be difficult for some believers, but sometimes listening can be much more difficult! Listening to people can involve hearing their impressions or observations of us. This can be an extremely painful experience as the raw nerve ends of our needs are exposed! Have you recently defended yourself with excuses or explanations when your spouse or co-worker is being honest with you? It is important to learn to listen, because only then can we understand what God desires and how we should respond to Him. Proverbs 8:33 says, "Hear instruction, and be wise, and refuse it not."

Our ability to construct a facade for ourselves is amazing. The facade we build may be the appearance of appreciative and careful attention, while inside [and out of sight of the speaker] we are suffering the agony of rejection and failure.

We are often afraid to listen because of what we might come to understand about ourselves. So much of our listening can be clouded with fear and anxiety. Did you grow up listening to harsh, abusive speech? If so, you may have a difficult time listening to helpful criticism or loving correction now. The fear and suspicion that enter our minds when we are young form a grid through which we pass all that is said to us as adults. Now perhaps we feel personal ministry is only an indictment of our failure. However, take heart; we can be free to listen without fear and without being overcome with a sense of failure. If we understand that we are securely positioned in Christ, we will have confidence and assurance that our relationship with God cannot be changed and His acceptance of us cannot be dampened.

When we experience this pain and sense of failure, it is especially difficult for us to see pride as our root problem. After all, we feel anything but proud! Yet, protecting and defending ourselves means that our heart's focus is not on the Lord and who He is, but on ourselves and who we are.

"Slow to Speak"

Too often it is our opinion, not God's, that we are quick to express. When we speak, we have usually reached a conclusion or at least, have an opinion. Perhaps James here encourages us not to be hasty in reaching a conclusion or in voicing our opinion too soon. It is not actually *time* that is the issue here, but *attitude*. In other words, it is not so important whether we listen one minute or one hour before we speak; the important thing is that we listen with a sense of needing God to help us to understand, and needing His wisdom in forming a conclusion. If we are self-confident and sure of our own ability to sort out the problem, then we will be quick to speak or give our opinion and slow to listen or wait upon God for understanding.

Speaking Should Follow Listening

It is certainly not the purpose of this chapter to compare speaking with listening, or to value one above another. God has given us the ability to do both and intends for us to grow and mature in the use of each. However, possibly we are more concerned about our speaking abilities than our listening sensitivity. Perhaps we could say we are more eager to speak than to listen because we rightly see the importance of expressing ourselves but wrongly miss the importance of listening with a view to understanding. We could generally say, speaking follows listening; that is, we should first understand what needs to be said before we try to say it. Proverbs 18:13 says, "He that answereth a matter before he heareth it, it is folly and shame unto him." Often, we begin to speak before we listen and because we have not taken the opportunity to understand before we speak, we cause painful confrontations or misunderstandings.

Don't Be Hasty or Hesitant

When God's Word cautions us to be slow to speak, it is not saying that we should be hesitant to speak because of fleshly timidity. We must not be hesitant to say what God prompts us to say; in fact, we are to speak with boldness or confidence. Paul asked prayer for himself that he would speak boldly as he "ought to speak" and that he might "open (his) mouth boldly, to make known the mystery of the gospel" (Eph. 6:19-20).

However, the secret of Paul's boldness was the confidence that he was saying what God wanted him to say. He wrote in 1 Thessalonians 2:4, "But as we were allowed of God to be put in trust with the gospel, even so we speak; not as pleasing men, but God, which trieth our hearts." If we pride ourselves in the notion that we speak our mind, we might simply be proud of ourselves! We must speak God's mind, not our own; to know His mind, we must listen to know what He would have us say. When our hearts are right with God, we speak boldly and without hesitancy. Proverbs 28:1 encourages us in this truth by saying, "The righteous are bold as a lion."

Our Speaking Should Direct Others to Christ

Our speaking should not reflect the world's attitudes of ungodliness and unbelief, no matter what pressures others put upon us. There are occasions when the wrong actions or attitudes of others can be exasperating, but this is exactly when we should be "slow to speak." If we speak when exasperated, we will be communicating not God's attitudes but our own fleshly ones. The results of our exasperation could be more damaging than the original problem. Moses found the children of Israel to be very frustrating with their rebellious attitudes and behavior. At what came to be called "the waters of Meribah," Moses paid dearly for his haste in speaking.

This account is given in Psalm 106:32-33 —

"They angered him also at the waters of strife, so that it went ill with Moses for their sakes, because they provoked his spirit, so that he spake unadvisedly with his lips." When Moses spoke his rash and hasty words, "Hear now, ye rebels; must we fetch you water out of this rock?" (Num. 20:10), and hit the rock, he did not glorify God nor set Him apart in the eyes of the children of Israel as the only one who could supply their needs. Christ is still God's only provision for us and for those who might exasperate us by unbelief and rebellion. If we react with rash words, we are not directing that person's attention to Christ.

"Slow to Wrath"

Wrath Among Believers

Quickness to wrath has caused problems among believers since the beginning days of the church up to the present time. When Paul anticipated his first visit to Corinth in 2 Corinthians 12:20, he expressed concern that he would find the Christians involved in "debates, envyings, wraths, strifes, backbitings, whisperings, swellings, (and) tumults." To the Ephesian church Paul wrote, "Let all bitterness, and wrath, and anger, and clamour, and evil speaking, be put away from you, with all malice" (Eph. 4:31). To the Colossian believers Paul had similar words: "But now ye also put off all these; anger, wrath, malice, blasphemy, filthy communication out of your mouth" (Col. 3:8). When we examine some of these words found in Colossians more closely, we realize the devastating effect we can have on other believers if we are quick to walk in the flesh. *Anger* is the intention to get revenge. *Wrath* is a boiling agitation of the feelings that can suddenly burst forth. *Malice* is the desire to injure. *Blasphemy* is slander or speech that injures another person's name.

Haste Makes Waste

Here is a time that this little saying is true! Our haste to speak our mind is foolish and wasteful, as Proverbs 14:29 says: "He that is slow to wrath is of great understanding: but he that is hasty of spirit exalteth folly." The blessing of being slow to speak and slow to wrath is that we won't provide opportunity for the devil to cause divisions among us. Proverbs 15:1 says, "A soft answer turneth away wrath: but grievous words stir up anger." We can turn away wrath or stir it up according to the words we speak. If we stir it up, we must conclude that we are given to wrath, or in other words, easily led about by the old nature. It is no good excusing ourself by blaming the other person.

Proverbs 15:18 says, "A wrathful man stirreth up strife: but he that is slow to anger appeaseth strife." How important is it to be slow to wrath? Proverbs 16:32 claims that it is more important than military genius! "He that is slow to anger is better than the mighty; and he that ruleth his spirit than he that taketh a city." In the spiritual battle we are engaged in together, wouldn't slowness to anger be of more value than all the skills and abilities we may have acquired to do missionary work?

The Weapon of Our Speech

If we are quick to speak, perhaps it is an indication that we are being easily led about by the old nature. Paul writes in Romans 6:12-13 "Let not sin therefore reign in your mortal body, that ye should obey it in the lusts thereof. Neither yield ye your members as instruments of unrighteousness unto sin: but yield yourselves unto God."

Our faculty of speech is included in "our members," which we can yield to be used as instruments of righteousness or unrighteousness. The word *instruments* was used by the Greeks to refer to the weapons of the Greek soldier. Paul was teaching us that the members of our body can be used in our warfare against evil. It is a tragedy when we yield the members of our body to the flesh and they become weapons of unrighteousness that we turn against one another.

"The Wrath of Man Worketh Not the Righteousness of God"

The Destruction Caused by Man's Wrath

When we listen to one another, it is important to understand not only what the speaker is saying, but what God is saying. In other words, we should have as our heart's desire and determination to understand what is right and just in God's sight. Our fleshly emotions will never lead us to godly conclusions. Cain was a man who was led by his fleshly emotions to disastrous consequences. When God rejected Cain and Cain's bloodless sacrifice of fruit and vegetables, we read, "Cain was very wroth" (Gen. 4:5). He would not humble himself before God but persisted in his anger, until one day while talking with his brother in the field, "Cain rose up against Abel his brother, and slew him" (Gen. 4:8). This is the first mention of man's wrath recorded in the Bible and in human history. This is very significant because it shows us clearly that man's wrath will undoubtedly result in the destruction of the well-being of ourselves and others.

Three Things to Avoid

There are at least three things we should avoid in listening to each other, things that will not result in the righteousness of God.

1. Listening With an Unforgiving Spirit

Our emotions often involve our anger at what a person has said or done to hurt us in the past.

It is extremely dangerous for us to carry these things in our hearts; when we listen to one another, our sinful, unforgiving attitudes will form a confusing grid of bias and we will interpret whatever is said to us as another attempt to hurt us. God has made it clear how we must handle the bitterness, anger, and wrath that may enter into our hearts because of problems in our relationships. In Ephesians 4:32 God says, "And be ye kind one to another, tenderhearted, forgiving one another, even as God for Christ's sake hath forgiven you." We must always allow room for God to work in each other's lives and the spiritual growth that results. We must not assume that a person's attitudes and motives are the same today as they were in the past.

2. Listening Without Meekness

One of the hardest times for us to listen to other people is when they are obviously wrong in their thinking and are expressing wrong attitudes and opinions. It is so easy for us to point to a person's wrong thinking in such a judgmentally severe and devastating way that a confrontation results, or the person refuses to say any more about it. If this occurs, we could excuse ourselves by saying it is "his problem," but it would be far better to see our wrong in not keeping the door of communication open so that we can keep listening to his response and help him toward right thinking. Regrettably, many of us as believers cannot handle opportunities like this without confrontation, and a relationship problem results. Perhaps what we lack is the spirit of meekness that Galatians 6:1 encourages us to have. "Brethren, if a man be overtaken in a fault, ye which are spiritual, restore such an one *in the spirit of meekness*; considering thyself, lest thou also be tempted" (italics added).

3. Listening to Gossip

At times, we have made the mistake of listening second- or third-hand; that is, instead of listening to a person directly, we listen to what someone says about them or "what someone says someone says about them." This is like listening to someone's attempt to give someone's attempt to mimic the song of a white-throated sparrow and then making a judgment on what it sounds like. How can we possibly know what someone is really feeling inside if we don't listen to them directly? If we listen to gossip, we will become involved in spreading it ourselves. Gossip originates from the wrath of man, not the righteousness of God. It is called whispering in the New Testament and is associated in 2 Corinthians 12:20 with such evils as wrath, strife, and backbiting. The result of listening to gossip and spreading it by our own speech is misrepresentation, misunderstanding, and eventually, division. Proverbs 16:27-28 says, "An ungodly man diggeth up evil: and in his lips there is as a burning fire. A froward man soweth strife: and a whisperer separateth chief friends."

Conclusion

It is striking that Paul puts such emphasis on the gentle, godly qualities that make for harmony in our relationships.

First Timothy 6:11 says that we are to "follow after righteousness, godliness, faith, love, patience, meekness," and 2 Timothy 2:22 tells us to "follow righteousness, faith, charity, peace."

The blessings of having these qualities in our relationships cannot be measured; and the way to follow after them is to be swift to listen.

Chapter Seventeen

GATEWAYS INTO THE HEART

"Ye see the distress that we are in, how
Jerusalem lieth waste, and the gates
thereof are burned with fire" (Neh. 2:17).

When Nehemiah arrived at the ruins of Jerusalem, he went out one night to view the rubble in anticipation of rebuilding. As he traveled slowly around the city in the darkness, he was especially struck with two things: The walls were broken down and the gates were burned by fire. To his eye, the situation was clear; without gates there was no protection for the city. As we view our lives, like Nehemiah viewed Jerusalem, we might realize we are in distress in a spiritual sense and that we need to rebuild and strengthen the gates that lead into our hearts.

The Senses of Hearing and Sight Are Gateways Into Our Hearts

"Doth not the ear try words? and the mouth taste his meat?" (Job 12:11).

We understand that our mouths are the way by which food gets into our stomachs. Our taste buds are located in our mouth, and when we take a bite of food, these taste sensors will tell us immediately whether we like it or not. If we like it we swallow, and it goes into our stomachs. If it isn't good or suitable to our taste, then we don't have to swallow it or take any more next time! In much the same way, your ears "taste" the words you hear and we could say that our eyes "taste" the things we see. The word *try* from Job 12:11 means "to prove or test" and indicates a *choice*. We can choose not to continue listening to or looking at some things, and we can always choose whether we will give approval and assent to the things we must hear or see.

Our ears and eyes are like openings into our hearts and minds. As the door to your house gives access into your home, so your ears and eyes give access into your mind and heart. Would you open the door of your house and allow all the creatures of the jungle to come in as they wished? We make entryways as secure as possible against intruders who would do harm. Why then do we carelessly allow our ears to hear things and our eyes to see things that are evil and that can only work spiritual and moral havoc in our hearts? Once the creatures of the jungle got in your house, imagine how hard it would be to get them out!

We may say, "Well, I'm pretty careful about what I listen to and what I watch. The door is closed tight enough, I think. There may be a few cracks, but surely nothing big can get in." We are usually cautious when confronted with big or extreme changes to our thinking concerning what is right and what is wrong; but we are far more tolerant when changes come to us in small doses. It is this tolerance that presents a crack in the gate that eventually widens, giving access to more and more compromise. It's not only the big things that destroy us; rather, it is the little things we compromise on that break down our reserve.

A missionary in Senegal built a door on his house but neglected a small threshold for the door to fit tightly against at the bottom. A lion could not have gotten through the doorway, but during the night a poisonous snake slithered under the door! In the same manner evil can slither into our hearts.

God Created the Senses for His Purposes

"The hearing ear, and the seeing eye, the Lord hath made even both of them" (Prov. 20:12).

The Lord has a purpose for everything He has made. The first words that man's ears ever heard were those spoken by his Creator, blessing him and giving him instructions. "And God blessed them, and God said unto them, Be fruitful, and multiply, and replenish the earth, and subdue it: and have dominion ... but of the tree of the knowledge of good and evil, thou shalt not eat of it: for in the day that thou eatest thereof thou shalt surely die" (Gen. 1:28; 2:17).

The first thing that man's eyes looked upon was the perfect creation of God. When God saw everything He had made, He said it was "very good" (Gen. 1:31). What Adam saw — trees, the sea, the animals — he named, and the woman God gave to him could only make him worship and praise the Creator of all these wonders. God never intended that the eyes and ears of man should be a means whereby man was and is tempted to sin against his Creator. However, what God created for His purposes, Satan immediately set about to misuse.

Temptation First Came to Man Through the Gates of Ear and Eye

"Ye shall not surely die" (Gen. 3:4).

How foolish we are to forget that Satan reached the heart of Eve through her ears and through her eyes. It is the same way that he seeks to tempt our hearts to sin today. How subtly he approached Eve, speaking words sounding sympathetic and caring and even seeming to shed light on her situation. He explained to her by lies why God had commanded her not to eat of the fruit and how she really wouldn't die if she ate it. In fact, eating of the fruit would be good for her, a wise thing to do! And now as she looked on the fruit, Eve saw it in a way she had never seen it before. Having opened her ear gate to Satan, she was ready to open the gateway of her eyes. Looking at the tree *from Satan's point of view*, she found it was "pleasant to the eyes" and she strongly desired it in her heart, believing it would make her wise (Gen. 3:6). Remember, all that is desirable is not of God. Satan has continually spoken subtle lies that are presented to man as a "new and more progressive way." Listening to Satan's lies, man begins to feel enlightened, intelligent, and educated. He begins to look with pity and disdain upon those who simply choose to believe God. He considers them naive and fancies himself as wise, smart, and going places. He does not realize how he has been deceived and set up by Satan for a tragic fall.

How does this apply to missionaries giving themselves to serving God, often growing physically and mentally weary, simply doing what needs to be done? Perhaps our legitimate need for rest and relaxation provides our ENEMY with the opportunity that he needs. *Enter the Video!* This is not a book against videos, nor is it an attempt to put a legalistic ban on the use of them. However, it is a plea to consider how our sense of right and wrong and our desire for knowing God can be dulled if we carelessly take in a heavy dose of the entertainment provided by movie producers who don't necessarily have God's interests in mind. We must be discriminating about what we take in. Often we don't even seem to consider what God would have us do. We just choose on the basis of our desires.

We Have a Choice Concerning the Things We Hear and See

"And Lot lifted up his eyes, and beheld all the plain of Jordan..." (Gen. 13:10). "And the Lord said unto Abram ... Lift up now thine eyes, and look" (Gen. 13:14).

In these two verses we have a contrast for Lot and his uncle, Abram. We read that "Lot lifted up his eyes and beheld" a well-watered plain near the cities of wicked Sodom. What Lot's eyes beheld seemed to promise both success and security. There is not one indication that Lot sought the will of God or even wanted to know what God had in mind for him. As soon as Lot had departed, we read that the Lord appeared to Abram with these words: "Lift up now thine eyes, and look from the place where thou art northward, and southward, and eastward, and westward: for all the land which thou seest, to thee will I give it" (vv. 14-15).

Notice these contrasts and consider how they might apply to you:

    1. Lot looked and chose on the basis of his own desires, while Abram looked in obedience to God.

    2. What Lot saw, he went about to get for himself; what Abram saw, he believed God would give to him.

3. What Lot saw took his heart's desire away from God; in fact, he had been set up by Satan to live in Sodom; what Abram saw drew him in fellowship to God; in fact, he walked *with* God throughout the length and breadth of the land.

Lot could well be a picture of many of us. He did not realize how much Satan was using the gate of his eye to persuade his heart to go after what God had not given him. A lack of sensitivity and care concerning what God wants is the sad commentary on humanity today.

Man Has Turned His Senses Away From God

"For the time will come when they will not endure sound doctrine; but after their own lusts shall they heap to themselves teachers, having itching ears; and they shall turn away their ears from the truth, and shall be turned unto fables" (2 Tim. 4:3-4).

We could say man is seeking to tune God out. God the Creator has given man ears to hear what He has to say, but man is refusing to listen to God's truth; in fact, man is finding instructors who tell him lies that he wants to hear. The word *heap* means "to accumulate in piles," and there is no lack of people who will tell man what his sinful heart wants to hear. The verse says that people will "turn away their ears from the truth." This means more than simply turning the ears away once. It also means that these men will see to it that their ears are always in such a position that they will never hear truth.

The ear gate leads to the heart and mind, and man does not want to think about or consider the truth of God, which would most certainly convict him of his ways and motives. No wonder the very next words in the text are words of caution to believers, "But watch thou in all things" (2 Tim. 4:5).

Why do we Christians need to watch? Because Satan will seek to get us to listen to these false teachers with their educated foolishness. He is constantly bombarding our eyes and our ears with an attempt to turn our hearts away from God. Satan wants to control what you give your attention to and is a master at making evil sound and look innocent, attractive, progressive, and intelligent.

In the midst of this increased attack upon our senses by Satan and this world, Christian workers cannot be neutral and just drift along with the current of what is acceptable or promoted according to the standards of this world.

God Wants to Have Our Ear

"And it shall be, if he say unto thee, I will not go away from thee; because he loveth thee and thine house, because he is well with thee; then thou shalt take an awl, and thrust it through his ear unto the door, and he shall be thy servant for ever. And also unto thy maidservant thou shalt do likewise" (Deut. 15:16-17).

When a Hebrew servant reached the seventh year of service to his master, he faced the choice to go out free or to continue to serve his master for life. If he chose service to his master, then before the judges the master pushed an awl through his earlobe, marking him as that master's servant forever.

Why the ear? Perhaps one reason is this, that the ear is for listening to the master and receiving instruction from him. The servant's ear was devoted to hearing the voice of the master and no other. If we lived in the days of the "awl and the ear," we would no doubt have occasion to see men and women in the marketplaces with the telltale hole in the earlobe. We would quickly identify them as persons having their senses inclined toward their master. How about us? Do we have our eyes and ears inclined toward God and His wishes? How desperate are we to grow in our knowledge of God? Proverbs 2:1-5 gives us counsel that applies as much today as it did when it was written under inspiration:

"My son, if thou wilt *receive* my words, and *hide* my commandments with thee; So that thou *incline* thine ear unto wisdom, and *apply* thine heart to understanding; Yea, if thou *criest* after knowledge, and *liftest* up thy voice for understanding; If thou *seekest* her as silver, and *searchest* for her as for hid treasures; Then shalt thou understand the fear of the Lord, and find the knowledge of God."

Notice the words God uses that express what it means for God to have our ear. If we fear God we will choose to hear and see what pleases Him, and we will choose to refuse those things which, by entering into our ear gate and eye gate, will work the havoc of dullness in our hearts and minds. David wrote in Psalm 101:3, "I will set no wicked thing before mine *eyes*: I hate the work of them that turn aside; it shall not cleave to me" (italics added).

Job said in Job 31:1, "I made a covenant with mine *eyes*: why then should I think upon a maid?" (italics added). Joseph also chose not to give over his senses to evil and temptation. When he was tempted by Potiphar's wife day after day, we read that "he *hearkened* not unto her, to lie by her, or to be with her" (Gen. 39:10, italics added).

Conclusion

"Let not the gates of Jerusalem be opened until the sun be hot; and while they stand by, let them shut the doors, and bar them" (Neh. 7:3).

We started this chapter with Nehemiah viewing the burned gates of Jerusalem and acknowledging the distress the city was in. Nehemiah knew what to do and set about to repair the gates, thus providing protection for the city. But Nehemiah not only saw the need to repair the gates, he also recognized the importance of controlling those gates once they were repaired! He did not leave the gates open all night, and when they were shut, they were barred for security. If we would keep spiritually sharp and healthy, we must yield control of the gates of our eyes and ears to God and then depend upon Him to protect our hearts and minds from the entrance of evil.

Chapter Eighteen

THE GREED OF GEHAZI

> "He that is greedy of gain troubleth his own house; but he that hateth gifts shall live" (Prov. 15:27).

Gehazi was serving the prophet Elisha when he was caught up in greed. His New Testament counterpart, Demas, served with the apostle Paul when love for the world stole his heart from God. It would be a sad task to number the many servants of God who have been overtaken with greed, even in our lifetime alone. If Gehazi, who witnessed the power of God through the prophet's miracles, could fall, could not we also? The record is in 2 Kings 5:20-27.

Gehazi's Plans

"I will run after him, and take somewhat of him" (2 Kings 5:20).

All sin in our lives begins by taking root in our hearts. When we see corn begin to come up out of the ground, we can be sure that in the soil and out of sight are the plant's roots. Before the plant showed itself above ground, the roots were spreading and establishing themselves in the soil. Jesus said in Luke 12:15, "Take heed and beware of covetousness" *Covetousness* means "a wish for more," and this identifies the root that began to spread and take hold in Gehazi's heart. Of course, it is not wrong to wish to improve upon our situation as God provides, but to wish for more than God has given is greed. The root of greed can begin to spread in many areas of life. Achish was greedy for clothing and riches as he saw the Babylonian garment and wedge of silver. David was greedy for another man's wife as he watched Bathsheba from a distance. Haman's greed was for power and position as he sought to destroy Mordecai and the Jews. We don't know how long Gehazi was nursing a discontentment in his heart, but we must be sure of one thing: Any evil desire that is teased and tolerated will in time develop into active pursuit.

Gehazi's Pursuit

"So Gehazi followed ... running" (2 Kings 5:21).

Proverbs 6:18 says that God hates "feet that be swift in running to mischief." Gehazi's feet were swift in pursuing the mischief his heart had planned. He no longer desired to wait on Elisha; he thought only of what he could get for himself.

The New Testament word for *follow* as used in 2 Timothy 2:22 brings out the meaning of "intense pursuit." The verse says, "Flee also youthful lusts: but follow righteousness, faith, charity, peace, with them that call on the Lord out of a pure heart." In this verse fleeing is a negative necessity, and following is a positive opportunity. There will always be a need for flight, even as there is always an opportunity to follow.

We cannot possibly do both at the same time! Gehazi could only run in one direction, and he ran the wrong way. The closer Gehazi got to Naaman's silver, the stronger became his resolve to get some for himself. We simply do not become stronger by refusing to flee temptation.

We must not entertain sinful thought as a guest in our hearts or allow our feet to take us into compromising situations. Like Gehazi, we will find ourselves picking up speed until we are at a dead run toward completing the sinful act our hearts have already been sinful in entertaining.

Gehazi's Lie

"My master hath sent me" (2 Kings 5:22).

This is one of the oldest and most widely used excuses for sin and disobedience the world has ever known. In order to cover his wish for more, Gehazi gave his greed a spiritual tone. We all have heard it and perhaps have even said it ourselves. In place of "my master hath sent me" we say, "I feel that this is what God wants me to do." There is nothing wrong, of course, in saying either one; in fact, it is our highest privilege to do so. However, let us be sure we are being honest and not deceitful.

Lying is a natural companion of greed. They are never far apart; in fact, where you see one, you most certainly can see the other lurking in the shadows if you look. For man to fulfill his selfish desires, he must lie and cheat. Ephesians 4:19 tells us of people "who being past feeling have given themselves over ... to work all uncleanness with greediness." Sin produces a moral numbness and insensibility in our hearts and minds. As Gehazi approached Naaman's chariot, he was "past feeling" and lied without a twinge of pain in his conscience.

The effectiveness of a lie depends on how close it appears to the truth. Certainly Gehazi's lie sounded logical and possible, and besides that, he had caught Naaman in the happy and thankful condition of just being healed from his dreaded leprosy. How glad, then, he would be to give of his riches and continue on his way rejoicing in his healing! In our ministry of involvement with people, we must guard against taking advantage of their thankfulness and appreciation. Spiritual blessings are free to all who will take them. The healing of Naaman's leprosy was a picture of the salvation and cleansing from sin provided free to sinners by the grace of God. Gehazi violated that provision by greedily seeking benefit for himself.

Gehazi's Seeming Success

"Take two talents ... with two changes of garments" (2 Kings 5:23).

Gehazi's deceitful plan had seemingly been pulled off without a hitch! When Naaman had offered him two talents of silver instead of just the one he asked for, Gehazi had managed to control his greed just enough to be urged before finally accepting the gift. A talent weighed about one hundred pounds, or all that a man could normally carry, so the total of two hundred pounds of silver represented a lot of wealth.

With his servants dismissed and the silver and clothing safely hidden away, Gehazi joined countless others down through the ages who have deluded themselves by thinking, *Who will know? Who will find out?*

Sin carries with it an appearance of success, and for a time sin seems to have no consequences. The writer of Psalm 73 confessed, "I was envious at the foolish, when I saw the prosperity of the wicked" (v. 3). Maybe we are having a hard time relating to the seeming success of Gehazi's sin because we have never run after a man just healed from leprosy and come away with two hundred pounds of silver! Remember, it is greed we are thinking about, and we can be greedy about many things! Money, things, position, pleasure, comfort, recognition, popularity, acceptance — the list could go on endlessly. The things we are greedy for are not in themselves sinful, and when God gives them to us they are a blessing; but when we run after them because of discontentment, we are showing our dissatisfaction with God and how He supplies for us.

It is not that we cannot get what we want if we set our minds to it. It is scary to think of, but all our scheming and conniving can actually secure for us what we are determined to have. We can manipulate co-workers, committees, and situations until things work out the way we desire, but there is no ultimate success in sin. The writer of Psalm 73, after spending time with God concerning the seeming success of the ungodly, said, "Then understood I their end" (v. 17). It is the *end* we are interested in and for Gehazi, it was a miserable end that loomed unavoidably before him.

Gehazi's Exposure

"Whence comest thou, Gehazi?" (2 Kings 5:25)

Gehazi had just hidden his treasures and calmly walked into Elisha's presence to resume his duties as though nothing was wrong. There have been many cases exposed where men and women in Christian ministry continue to live in sin — immorality, adultery, theft, and deceit — but still carry out their daily ministry as though all is well. This may go on for weeks, months, or even years before it is finally brought to light. It was Gehazi's obvious intention to have his sin and service too. In answer to Elisha's searching question, he managed a feeble lie: "Thy servant went no whither" (v. 25). But it was no good; God had given discernment to Elisha that had followed Gehazi's every move like a hidden video camera. Hebrews 4:13 says, "Neither is there any creature that is not manifest in his sight: but all things are naked and opened unto the eyes of him with whom we have to do." We cannot toy with the uncompromising standard of God's holiness. He will not permit us to continue in sin without exposure. It is only a matter of time before the truth of Numbers 32:23 is apparent: "Be sure your sin will find you out."

This is not to say there is not grace and forgiveness with God, provided through the shed blood of His beloved Son. Let every Christian know we have access into grace through our Lord Jesus Christ (see Rom. 5:1-2)! "If we confess our sins, he is faithful and just to forgive us our sins, and to cleanse us from all unrighteousness" (1 John 1:9). There is no reason, except our own pride, that we should continue one moment out of fellowship with God.

As surely as Elisha's first question exposed Gehazi's sin, his second question revealed the foolishness and wrong of it. "Is it a time to receive...?" (2 Kings 5:26). Is it a time for us as Christian workers to greedily grasp after the silver and garments of this world that are soon to perish? First Peter 4:7 says, "But the *end* of all things is at hand: be ye therefore sober, and watch unto prayer" (italics added). Second Peter 3:11 says, "Seeing then that all these things shall be dissolved, what manner of persons ought ye to be?"

Gehazi's Judgment

"And he went out from his presence a leper" (2 Kings 5:27).

Little did Gehazi realize that the silver and the

garments which he had longed for and pursued were contaminated with the leprosy of Naaman! How true Galatians 6:7 is shown to be. "Be not deceived; God is not mocked: for whatsoever a man soweth, that shall he also reap." To have leprosy was bad, but worse yet are the words, "He went out from his presence"! Gehazi lost his wonderful opportunity to serve God in this way and could no longer assist Elisha. The ENEMY does not give us a detailed breakdown of what our greed will cost us if we yield to it. Take for example, the greed that results in adultery or immorality. The enemy will only whisper about the pleasure not the pain, but look for a moment at the pain: the grief and mistrust suffered by your spouse; the lifelong scars of memory; the harmful effects on your children; your soiled testimony before co-workers and supporters; your sorrow and embarrassment in getting on the plane to return home to face family, relatives, and church family; perhaps the impossibility of returning to ministry; your responsibility in bringing sorrow and pain to the other guilty party; the knowledge of having sinned against the Lord who loves you so much.

These are not pleasant things to consider, but it is far better to consider them than to suffer them! Leprosy was certainly not on Naaman's mind as he raced greedily after Naaman's chariot, but if he knew that was what he was running after, his pursuit might have turned to flight.

The admonition of Hebrews 13:5 is good for our hearts to feast upon in light of what we have considered. "Let your conversation be without covetousness; and be content with such things as ye have: for he hath said, I will never leave thee, nor forsake thee."

Chapter Nineteen

PURITY IS PRIORITY

"But the wisdom that is from above is
first pure" (James 3:17).

Of the various aspects of God's wisdom, purity is said to be first, meaning that it takes priority. Regardless of this world's scorn of holiness and its passion for all that is vile, God still holds purity as priority. *Purity* means "free from defilement" or "free from contamination."

Experts are concerned about specific impurities in our physical environment like the air we breathe, the ozone layer, and our sources of fresh water, and they are very alert to identify the possible contaminants. In this chapter we consider six specific areas where our spiritual purity is threatened, and we seek to identify the sources of contamination.

Our Confidence in the Word of God and the Contamination of Human Wisdom

"The commandment of the Lord is pure, enlightening the eyes" (Ps. 19:8).

The Word of God is pure because it is solely God's words, having none of man's wisdom or philosophy mixed with it. Because it is pure, it alone can help us to see clearly through the haze and pollution of what man thinks. The Word of God enlightens us, removing our spiritual dullness and restoring us to alertness and "battle readiness."

Once when fighting against the Philistines, Saul very selfishly commanded the people not to take any nourishment until the battle was over! His son Jonathan did not hear this command of his father; as he went through a wooded area, he dipped his rod into a honeycomb, putting it to his mouth. Immediately he exclaimed, "See, I pray you, how mine eyes have been enlightened, because I have tasted a little of this honey" (1 Sam. 14:24-29). By his foolish command, Saul was causing his fighting men to become dull and weak, but just a little honey made Jonathan alert and restored his readiness for the fight.

Psalm 12:6 says, "The words of the Lord are pure words: as silver tried in a furnace of earth, purified seven times." Seven is the number of perfection, emphasizing that the words of God are perfect in their purity. With such an uncorrupted source of wisdom at our disposal, why should we turn elsewhere and neglect God's Word? When we are searching for understanding concerning an important matter, where do we turn for answers? If you wanted to know how to raise your children, how to have a happy marriage, or how to deal with the emotional hurts of your past, where would you turn? All too often we look for a good book on the subject by a well-known authority in that field. Man's words are certainly valuable but only as they direct the heart and mind of the reader to the pure words of God.

Our Worship of God and the Contamination of Idolatry

"And thou shalt love the Lord thy God with all thy heart, and with all thy soul, and with all thy mind, and with all thy strength" (Mark 12:30).

Should we naively suppose we are unaffected by the idolatry of the world around us? Paul wrote to the Corinthians in 1 Corinthians 10:14, "Wherefore, my dearly beloved, flee from idolatry." The Word of God would not warn us to flee something we are not in danger of. Consider where man directs his worship and see if we aren't in danger of being corrupted by similar attitudes.

    1. Man worships himself and his own well-being (John 12:25).

    2. Man worships objects he possesses or is lusting after (Matt. 6:32-33).

    3. Man worships other people, giving preference to them over God (Acts 12:21-23).

    4. Man worships images or likenesses of man and animals, even to the very lowest forms of life (Rom. 1:23).

In Mark 12:30, Jesus prefaced heart, soul, mind, and strength with the little word *all*, which simply brings out the meaning of totality. Any preference of ourselves, our possessions, or other people contaminates the purity of worship.

Isn't idolatry a primary cause of our lack of commitment to serving God unreservedly? Why does it take so long for us to decide to do what God would have us do? Idolatry robs us of God's wisdom, making us hesitant and indecisive because of our divided love and affection.

Our Distinction as Believers and the Contamination of Compromise

"Thou art of purer eyes than to behold evil, and canst not look on iniquity" (Hab. 1:13).

Through our eyes we let things into our hearts, minds, and eventually, our lives. As we look, we look with approval or disapproval. God never looks upon evil with the slightest tolerance or approval; and because His wisdom is "first pure," it is not given to us if we approve of evil by an attitude of compromise. When we tolerate evil, we lose the sharp cutting edge of our witness for God.

That which is pure has the quality of being "without mixture." It will not tolerate any contaminant and does not blend with other substances. The child of God is meant to be without mixture, apart from the world about him.

We are pressured continually from all sides. Tragically, we would often prefer to compromise than be conspicuous. We are afraid to be without mixture because we don't want to be different, and we don't want to stand alone. We feel we must compromise just a little so we can fit in. However, we cannot fit in because we are pieces of a different puzzle than this world. It is clear that compromise is not in God's plan for us, as He said in 2 Corinthians 6:17 "Be ye separate."

The Training of Our Young People and the Contamination of Change

"Even a child is known by his doings, whether his work be pure, and whether it be right" (Prov. 20:11).

Foundations are laid early in the construction of

any building. Failure to do so will cause structural damage to the building itself. Purity of life should begin at childhood. Because we cannot go with our children all through their lives, we seek to lay a foundation of purity in their hearts and minds that will allow them to apply God's wisdom to life's vital decisions.

There seems to be a growing philosophy among Christian leaders that may permit contamination and rob us of God's wisdom. It is the philosophy that we live in the '90s — times have changed, our world has changed, and our young people have changed — therefore we must change our approach in raising them, training them, and preparing them for God's service.

God hasn't changed; He has no need to change. It is the world that is sliding at breakneck speed away from an unchanging God.

After thousands of years of world history, after man has continually changed his moral standards to suit himself, Christ will come to set up his earthly kingdom and will rule with a "rod of iron" (Rev. 19:15). That doesn't sound like God has changed!

We must acknowledge that our world definitely has changed and that we all, including our Christian young people, are affected by that change, but what wisdom would God give us to know what to do? The answer is to lay solid foundations from the Word of God concerning *who God is and what He is like*. This will definitely work a change — not a change of conformity to this world, but a change of submission toward God and love and worship toward Him.

Our Relationship With One Another and the Contamination of Sinful Attitudes

"Seeing ye have purified your souls in obeying the

truth through the Spirit unto unfeigned love of the brethren, see that ye love one another with a pure heart fervently" (1 Pet. 1:22).

It is more and more acceptable in our Christian society to "work through" wrong attitudes toward people. Psychology says that it takes time to be able to forgive someone and let go of our anger and bitterness. It seems that as long as we are working at it, we are doing all that can be expected. However, God's Word says, "Let all bitterness, and wrath, and anger ... be put away from you, with all malice ... forgiving one another" (Eph. 4:31-32).

It is impossible to be right with God if we are not right with each other. If we harbor wrong attitudes, we cannot say we love each other, and if we do not love each other, we cannot say we love God. "If a man say, I love God, and hateth his brother, he is a liar: for he that loveth not his brother whom he hath seen, how can he love God whom he hath not seen?" (1 John 4:20). If we do not maintain godly attitudes and deal with our wrong ones, then we cannot conduct ourselves with wisdom in our relationships, and many problems will result.

Our Motive For Living and the Contamination of Self-Glory and Self-Seeking

"Beloved, now are we the sons of God, and it doth not yet appear what we shall be: but we know that, when he shall appear, we shall be like him; for we shall see him as he is. And every man that hath this hope in him purifieth himself, even as he is pure" (1 John 3:2-3).

The hope and expectation of being with Him for eternity has a purifying effect upon our lives; that is, it causes us to reject self-glory and self-seeking and to live only for His glory. Our motivation for time should be the same as our motivation for eternity — His glory, not our own. Any other motivation is a contamination and clouds our service with selfish ambition. Because God's wisdom is "first pure," it is not given to those who would use it for their own selfish ends. If we live for men's praise, we can certainly obtain it, but only for this life. In the end we will take nothing with us because man's glory does not follow him into eternity. "Be not thou afraid when one is made rich, when the glory of his house is increased; for when he dieth he shall carry nothing away: his glory shall not descend after him. Though while he lived he blessed his soul: and men will praise thee, when thou doest well to thyself" (Ps. 49:16-18). In 1 Timothy 5:22, Paul admonished Timothy with three words: "Keep thyself pure." If we combine 1 Timothy 5:22 with James 3:17, we realize the importance of purity: "Keep thyself pure," for "the wisdom that is from above is first pure."

Chapter Twenty

LET THERE BE NO STRIFE

> "And Abram said unto Lot, Let there be
> no strife, I pray thee, between me and
> thee, and between my herdmen and thy
> herdmen; for we be brethren"
> (Gen. 13:8).

These words of Abram in Genesis 13:8 were said to his nephew Lot because strife had broken out between their herdmen. We borrow it to apply its principle to our lives as brothers and sisters in the Lord. The problem between the herdmen developed because of material abundance. Together their flocks and herds were so great that the land could not sustain them. The tragic problem is summarized in verse 6: "They could not dwell together." How strange that God's blessings should cause strife among God's people! How devastating is the encroachment of materialism into our fellowship. How tragic if it must be said of us, "They could not work together!"

Strife and *contention* are two words used in Proverbs to refer to conflicts in relationships. As we look at these verses in Proverbs we will dig deeper than the surface statement, "They just can't work together," and we will consider what might be the heart or core problem.

An Angry Heart

"A wrathful man stirreth up strife: but he that is slow to anger appeaseth strife" (Prov. 15:18).

Inside the heart of an angry person some inner turmoil is raging. Because of this inner turmoil, such a person cannot tolerate a restful or calm relationship with others.

What are some of the things that make us angry? Consider what prompted anger in the hearts of these three biblical characters:

   1. Joseph's brothers were filled with *envy and jealousy* at their favored brother and held a grudge that was waiting to be unleashed. Revenge was the driving force of their lives. They wanted to get back at their father for favoring Joseph, and they wanted to hurt Joseph because he was not wicked like them.

   2. Jonah's heart was *resentful and bitter* toward God because God had asked him to serve the hated and despised Ninevites. Instead of feeling merciful, he felt hatred and wanted to see them destroyed. Proverbs 10:12 says, "Hatred stirreth up strifes: but love covereth all sins."

   3. The Prodigal's brother was angry that his younger brother was given a celebration and he was not, even though it seemed he had never desired that kind of relationship with his father before. His anger was generated by his *hurt pride*. He was performance-oriented and based his relationship with his father on what he did for his father. When we do not understand our secure position in Christ, we, like this man, become angry at God; we can never seem to do

enough to satisfy our own pride and believe that we have attained a secure position in His favor.

A Proud Heart

"He that is of a proud heart stirreth up strife: but he that putteth his trust in the Lord shall be made fat" (Prov. 28:25).

Pride shows itself through two opposing attitudes — superiority and inferiority. A proud person is occupied with an evaluation of himself, whether that evaluation be good or bad. How easily pride deceives us into thinking our opinions, views, and ways are superior. Pride makes it impossible for us to accept others the way they are. To accept someone means we are no longer insisting that they change to be like us; we are content to trust God to do in their lives what He thinks best.

Our pride also appears through the resentment of feeling inferior to others and that our views and ways are really stupid and foolish. In either case, as Proverbs 13:10 says, "Only by pride cometh contention."

A person who feels inferior causes as much contention as a person who feels superior because in both cases, the heart is focused on self and not on the Lord who desires to be everything to us. It is frustrating to our team if we belittle our own God-given gifts and abilities and choose to live in an "I can't" world.

A Perverse Heart

"A froward man soweth strife: and a whisperer separateth chief friends" (Prov. 16:28).

The definition of *froward*, as used in Proverbs, carries the meaning of being perverse, or turning aside from that which is right and just.

Perverseness can be of action or of the mouth or speech, such as when a person twists the truth to misrepresent what someone else has said or done. Perhaps for this reason the froward man is also identified as a "whisperer" or a "talebearer" (Prov. 20:19).

There are three things needed to keep a fire going: fuel, heat, and oxygen. Fire fighters seek to remove one or more of these elements in fighting fires. If we liken strife to an unwanted fire, we can liken the contentious man, perverse in his speech, to the fuel. Proverbs 26:20-21 completes the picture: "Where no wood is, there the fire goeth out: so where there is no talebearer, the strife ceaseth. As coals are to burning coals, and wood to fire; so is a contentious man to kindle strife."

The speech of a contentious person is not trustworthy because of his tendency to inaccuracy and departure from the truth. Many relationship problems have been a result of misunderstanding caused by a contentious person misrepresenting what someone has said or done.

Clearly this is the reason why best friends are separated. A contentious person causes problems where there are no problems and can quickly turn a harmonious working relationship into one of suspicion and mistrust.

A Foolish Heart

"A fool's lips enter into contention, and his mouth calleth for strokes" (Prov. 18:6).

No one is more certain of his wisdom than a fool. For this reason he will freely give his opinions and offer his advice. If one word could characterize the actions of a fool, it might be the word *impulsiveness*. He is quick to jump into other people's problems, confident he has the answer at hand. Proverbs 25:8 warns us against such impulsiveness — "Go not forth hastily to strive, lest thou know not what to do in the end thereof, when thy neighbor hath put thee to shame."

Many times we enter into contention simply by talking too much. Proverbs 10:19 says, "In the multitude of words there wanteth not sin: but he that refraineth his lips is wise." A wise man under the control of the Spirit desires and is able to refrain (hold back or restrain) his lips, but a foolish man talks on and on without thought of the consequences of his words. He lacks the wisdom of the Spirit of God, and his words do not help to keep what Ephesians 4:3 calls "the unity of the Spirit." Contention and division are often the sad results.

A Scornful Heart

"Cast out the scorner, and contention shall go out; yea, strife and reproach shall cease" (Prov. 22:10).

A scorner is a person given to scoffing and belittling others. Such a person looks down on others from a precarious self-elevated height that can only be maintained by minimizing the efforts and accomplishments of others.

Have you ever been in a conversation with someone and found that the discussion continually returned to him or her and revolved around his or her accomplishments and activities?

Perhaps we should reverse the question and ask ourselves pointedly, "Do we do this to others?" We may not easily relate talking about ourselves as acting the part of a scorner, but in order to lift ourselves up we must minimize others, and this brings contention into our fellowship.

Proverbs 22:10 clearly links scorn and contention

together when it says, "Contention shall go out [with the scorner]." Diotrephes's love for preeminence would not permit him to receive the apostle John, because to allow the apostle to minister in the church would have threatened his own self-elevation. Instead, he belittled Paul, raising false accusations against him (see 3 John 9-10).

Scorning also appears as a pessimistic and negative attitude, which has the same effect as a cold drizzle on a much-desired campfire. A classic example is the scorner Tobiah, who belittled Nehemiah's hard work by saying, "Even that which they build, if a fox go up, he shall even break down their stone wall" (Neh. 4:3).

A Carnal Heart

"For ye are yet carnal: for whereas there is among you envying, and strife, and divisions, are ye not carnal, and walk as men?" (1 Cor. 3:3).

We have been looking at the contentious man from the book of Proverbs; now Paul, in his letter to the Corinthians, draws our considerations together and clearly identifies as carnal the believer who causes strife and divisions. Can we not confidently say that contentiousness is the result of carnality? Of the billions of people living in the world, there are but three classes: the Natural man is unsaved, lost in sin and spiritually dead; the Spiritual man is saved by God's grace and is living under the control of the Holy Spirit; the Carnal man is also saved by the grace of God but unlike the Spiritual man, who is under God's control, the Carnal person is governed and motivated by his human nature. What can you expect from the flesh? Galatians 5:19-21 gives a list of evils which includes strife. James 3:16 goes on to say that where we allow strife, we open wide the door to all the other evils. "For where envying and strife is, there is confusion and every evil work."

Some Final Thoughts

In the matter of strife and contention, we cannot use the solution that Abram and Lot chose to accommodate sheep and cattle! To some, this might still seem the easiest way, as it is expressed in Genesis 13:9 — "Separate thyself, I pray thee, from me."

Perhaps we have identified ourselves as being angry, proud, perverse, foolish, or scornful. If so, it is vital to see the simplicity of our solution in Christ. If our lives bring strife and contention, are we not carnal? We, therefore, are not walking in fellowship with God, nor are we under the control of His Holy Spirit. There is no other solution than to humble ourselves before God and receive His forgiveness and cleansing. Our simple solution is found in the finished work of Christ, wherein we have fellowship with God and also freedom from the controlling power of our old nature.

Chapter Twenty-One

CHOOSING THANKFULNESS

"And let the peace of God rule in your
hearts, to the which also ye are called in
one body; and be ye thankful" (Col 3:15).

"First, I thank my God through Jesus Christ for you all, that your faith is spoken of throughout the whole world" (Rom. 1:8, italics added).

The word *first* speaks of priority or order of events; in other words, thankfulness should take priority as an attitude in our hearts toward others. What we first decide to think about one another sets the course for our future attitudes and actions. If we first decide to think impatiently or irritably, then that is how we will act toward others, and those wrong attitudes will continue to be manifest in our succeeding thoughts.

"First things first" is a well-known phrase and a principle brought out in the following illustrations:

    1. "*First* be reconciled to thy brother, and then come and offer thy gift" (Matt. 5:24, italics added).

2. "But seek ye *first* the kingdom of God, and his righteousness; and all these things shall be added unto you" (Matt. 6:33, italics added).

3. "The dead in Christ shall rise *first:* then we which are alive and remain shall be caught up." (1 Thess. 4:16-17, italics added).

God has His own priorities, and although Paul had many things to say to the Romans, he recognized the divine priority was to communicate thankfulness first. Sometimes believers are quick to be critical and faultfinding, and this seems to be a priority in how we view other people. It is not that we can't find things to be critical about, and certainly the ENEMY will assist us if we choose to be faultfinding. He can make little differences into mountains of separation, and he can haul old grievances out of the past for our review. We cannot expect to have a positive ministry in the lives of other people unless thankfulness takes priority in our attitudes toward them. When we lose this priority, we will most definitely communicate lack of appreciation, taking each other for granted, putting up with each other, etc.

Romans 1:8 gives us two facts about other believers that form a basis for making thankfulness for them priority:

1. The Priority of Position

Paul said, "I thank my God *through Jesus Christ* for you all." It was through Jesus Christ that salvation and security came to the believers. True, God had not finished with them yet, but that did not change the security of their position in Christ. We often put the cart before the horse in our relationships. We think that when people become easy to work with, more pleasant to be around, or change in some way, then we can be thankful for them. In other words, we insist upon change before thankfulness, but God insists upon thankfulness before change! As we relate to other believers we tend to see first *the weakness of their condition* rather than *the security of their position.* For this reason, we are always trying to force a change rather than resting in God's faithfulness to work in their lives.

2. The Priority of Witness

Paul said, "I thank my God... *that your faith is spoken of throughout the whole world."* The Roman believers' faith in God was being discussed by people all over the world, which glorified God because it revealed Him to be a living and trustworthy Creator. That our lives should bring glory to God is our highest calling and should make us thankful for each other. It is sometimes difficult to translate the tasks we do into glorifying God, but all of us as God's people are necessary as members of His BODY. First Corinthians 12:21-22 says, "The eye cannot say unto the hand, I have no need of thee:... those members of the body, which seem to be more feeble are necessary." We must be careful not to think wrongly about our lives. For example, it's possible for us to think that what we are doing brings more glory to God than what other members of the BODY are doing, or we can think the opposite and feel that what we are doing doesn't matter at all and God isn't even interested in it! If we think either of these thoughts, it is because our focus is on our own feeble attempts to do great things, not on God who is well able to glorify Himself through our lives. Paul said, "I have planted, Apollos watered; but God gave the increase" (1 Cor. 3:6).

Always — Maintaining Thankfulness in Our Daily Relationships

"I Thank my God *Always* on your behalf, for the grace of God which is given you by Jesus Christ: that in every thing ye are enriched by him, in all utterance, and in all knowledge" (1 Cor. 1:4-5).

Always means "at every season" and emphasizes the need to strive in the Spirit to maintain something; in this case, of course, the need is to maintain thankfulness. Notice the following two uses of this word:

>1. "Be ye stedfast, unmoveable, *always* abounding in the work of the Lord" (1 Cor. 15:58, italics added).
>
>2. "Giving thanks *always* for all things" (Eph. 5:20, italics added).

In both illustrations above we are encouraged to maintain something in spite of difficulties and discouragements, even though we might not feel like it. All our earthly relationships have difficulties that we must work through, but in doing so we must maintain a thankful attitude. Relationships are precious and worth working at; they don't just happen, and they certainly don't maintain themselves.

When we think of some of the hard things Paul had to say to the Corinthian believers, we might wonder whether he was really thankful for them. However, Paul maintained his thankfulness, even as he dealt with them concerning their need. How was he able to do this? Here is the secret: he was conscious that God's grace was extended to them. He said, "I thank my God ... *for the grace of God which is given you by Christ Jesus*." If God extends His grace toward other believers, should we not also?

Contrast some of the things Paul said to the Corinthians in his first letter to them that revealed their serious spiritual needs, with the words of encouragement he gave to them because he was confident of God's grace on their behalf.

<u>The Corinthians' Spiritual Needs</u>
1. "There are contentions among you" (1 Cor. 1:11).
2. "I ... could not speak unto you as unto spiritual, but as unto carnal" (3:1).
3. "It is reported commonly that there is fornication among you" (5:1).
4. "Now therefore there is utterly a fault among you, because ye go to law one with another" (6:7).

<u>God's Grace Extended to Them</u>
1. "Who shall also confirm you unto the end, that ye may be blameless in the day of our Lord Jesus Christ" (1:8).
2. "But of him are ye in Christ Jesus, who of God is made unto us wisdom, and righteousness, and sanctification, and redemption" (1:30).
3. "For we are labourers together with God: ye are God's husbandry, ye are God's building" (3:9).
4. "And such were some of you: but ye are washed, but ye are sanctified, but ye are justified in the name of the Lord Jesus" (6:11).

We must learn to evaluate the needs of our own lives and the lives of others through the wonderful grace of God. If we do not maintain thankfulness for God's grace extended toward ourselves and others, then all will look dark and hopeless, and discouragement will set in.

A Word in Season

Without Ceasing — Choosing Thankfulness in Spite of Difficulties:

"Wherefore I also, after I heard of your faith in the Lord Jesus, and love unto all the saints, *cease not* to give thanks for you, making mention of you in my prayers" (Eph. 1:15,16, italics added).

The words *cease not* emphasize a very important aspect of the Christian life which determines the quality of our relationships. It is the aspect of choice.

The fact that we can choose thankfulness as an attitude toward others can be applied very practically to our relationships. Thankfulness for others is always our choice. Whether I am thankful is not determined by someone else's choice. We can never say, "You made me ungrateful by what you said or did." In spite of external pressures it is always our responsibility and freedom to choose right attitudes. We have an illustration of this in Acts 5:40, 42.

"And when they had called the apostles, and beaten them, they commanded that they should not speak in the name of Jesus... and daily... they *ceased not* to teach and preach Jesus Christ" (italics added).

Do you adhere to the doctrine of the last straw? Do you ever feel that you have had enough of the way another person acts and resolve not to give them another chance? Has someone done something to you once too many times? Are you carrying hurts and bitterness in your heart toward those you should be thankful for? It is impossible to have both attitudes of unforgiveness and thankfulness at the same time. Like Peter, we wonder if there isn't a limit to how much we are required to forgive others. In Matthew 18:21 Peter asked, "Lord how oft shall my brother sin against me, and I forgive him?" However, as Jesus pointed out to Peter, our forgiveness of others should be limitless or "seventy times seven" (v. 22). Paul also made this abundantly clear when he said in Colossians 3:13, "Even as Christ forgave you, so also do ye."

Summary

Our attitudes toward others are like the building blocks of a foundation. We are building relationships; therefore, it is important to lay foundational blocks of thankfulness. A relationship built on suspicion, mistrust, bitterness, and resentment will eventually come crashing down during some tremor of difficulty. However, a relationship built upon and maintained by thankfulness will withstand the severest stress and trial.

Chapter Twenty-Two

PROVISIONS OF GRACE

> "Blessed be the Lord, who daily loadeth us with benefits, even the God of our salvation" (Ps. 68:19).

We usually think of the book of Jonah as the story of a man who tried to run away from God, yet it is also an account of God providing in grace what man needs.

We seldom know what we truly need, and we often resist God's provisions, sometimes even seeing them as inconveniences and hindrances to our plans.

God's provisions for us are always for His glory and our good, because our good is to bring glory to our Creator.

God Provided A Witness — Jonah

"Now the word of the Lord came unto Jonah" (Jon. 1:1).

Man can never say to God, "You never told me or sent anyone to tell me." All through the dispensations of time God has provided witnesses, although man has not always responded favorably to God, His message, or His messengers. God could have simply destroyed Nineveh. Instead He sent Jonah to "cry against it" (v. 2) so that the people would repent and He could provide salvation instead of sending judgment.

Actually, the prophet Jonah was sent with a message from God twice according to the Bible record. First, he was sent to Israel with a popular message and then to Nineveh with an unpopular one. To Israel, Jonah had the good news that prosperity was on the way. In 2 Kings 14:25 we read that a great amount of land was restored to Israel, "According to the word of the Lord God of Israel, which he spake by the hand of his servant Jonah." However, to Nineveh, Jonah's message was that judgment was on the way. "Yet forty days, and Nineveh shall be overthrown" (Jon. 3:4).

It is always easier to do what is popular than what is unpopular, to do what is pleasant than what is unpleasant, what is agreeable than what is disagreeable. To go to Israel was not only a popular and pleasant task, but to Jonah, it certainly was agreeable, as he wanted to see his nation prosper. To go to Nineveh was very dangerous and unpleasant, but more than that, it was disagreeable to Jonah, as he wanted to see Nineveh destroyed and didn't even want them to have the opportunity to repent of their evil ways. Because of his wrong attitude Jonah refused to obey God. When God said to Jonah, "Arise, go to Nineveh," he "rose up to flee" from the Lord (Jon. 1:2-3)

What about us? Are we willing to do the will of our Creator only when the task is popular and agreeable, or will we serve Him faithfully, even though the task is unpopular, unpleasant, and disagreeable?

Among the things that excite me most about heaven is what Revelation tells us we will be doing there! Cartoonists have given us a very faulty and unattractive (even boring), picture of heaven — those in heaven sitting on white fluffy clouds, playing small golden harps and gently fanning their wings. However, Revelation 22:3 makes us anticipate eagerly what awaits us: "The throne of God and of the Lamb shall be in it; *And His Servants Shall Serve Him*" (italics added). Think of it! We shall serve Him for evermore! This is worship that is active, challenging, and purposeful. Should we, then, ever think of fleeing from His commands during our few short years upon earth?

God Provided Correction — A Great Wind

"But the Lord sent out a great wind into the sea" (Jon. 1:4).

Because Jonah set his own course for his life, God in faithfulness set out to correct him. Jonah's course was purposeless and aimless. He had no goal in life except to avoid the course God had for him. God's course for each of us has its goal in eternity. God could have simply let Jonah go his own way, but he was as interested in Jonah as He was in those Assyrians in Nineveh.

As God had sent Jonah to Nineveh, so now He sent the wind after Jonah! Two word pictures from Scripture illustrate for us the greatness of God in having all creation at His command:

    1. Proverbs 30:4 says that God has "gathered the wind in his fists." We can easily imagine God gathering the wind in His hand and directing it with perfect accuracy toward the ship and runaway Jonah. Many years later, the disciples were to exclaim, "What manner of man is this, that even the wind and the sea obey him?" (Mark 4:41).

    2. Psalm 104:3 says God "walketh upon the wings of the wind." God who is omnipresent

was Himself traveling in the wind that He sent out.

Why did Jonah not want to go to Nineveh? There is no indication that he was afraid to go even though it was a dangerous mission. There is every indication that Jonah hated the Assyrian people for how they had hurt Israel.

Nineveh was the capital of Assyria, a nation that began about eight hundred years before Christ and whose armies terrorized Israel and other nations with ruthlessness and cruelty for over two hundred years. It was the Assyrians' practice to scatter their captives to prevent them from planning revolt. This is what Shalmaneser did to the northern kingdom of Israel, recorded for us in 2 Kings 18:11. "And the king of Assyria did carry away Israel unto Assyria, and put them in Halah and in Habor ... and in the cities of the Medes." Of course, families and loved ones would be separated, not only from their land, but from each other.

Perhaps the Assyrian king we know best is Sennacherib who sent his armies under Rabshakeh against the southern kingdom of Judah when Hezekiah was king. Sennacherib was the one who made Nineveh famous as his capital by building a wall forty to fifty feet high around a two-and-one-half-mile length next to the Tigris River. We are struck with the Assyrians' arrogance and rejection of God; Rabshakeh cried out to the Jews who were confined inside the walls of Jerusalem, "Neither let Hezekiah make you trust in the Lord, saying, the Lord will surely deliver us" (2 Kings 18:30). Two hundred years of domination and harassment by this godless nation had left its mark on all Jews, including Jonah. There were probably few, if any, nations or persons who would not have rejoiced to see suffering and pain come to Nineveh.

Although Jonah had his reasons for running, God

had His priorities for Jonah and for Nineveh. The correction of God is one of the sure evidences of His love and faithfulness. Hebrews 12:5-6 tells us to remember the words spoken many years before in Proverbs 3:11-12, "My son, despise not the chastening of the Lord; neither be weary of his correction: for whom the Lord loveth he correcteth; even as a father the son in whom he delighteth."

The book of Jonah is as much an account of God working in one life as it is of His working in many thousands of lives. God had committed Himself to warning the lost souls in Nineveh of His impending judgment *and* to teaching His servant Jonah obedience and compassion. We have good reason to say that God is as much concerned about what He can do *in* our lives as what He can do *through* them.

Hebrews 12:5-6 tells us there are two attitudes we are to be careful not to have when being corrected by God.

    1. We are not to despise chastening.

"Despise not thou the chastening of the Lord." The word despise comes from two words — *little* and *care*. It simply means we are not to think little or care little for God's correction. This would be like a foolish child who walks away from a spanking and says confidentially to his friend, "It didn't hurt much." What he is saying is, "I don't really care if I got spanked or not. I'll do what I want anyway!"

    2. We are not to faint when He rebukes us.

"Nor faint when thou art rebuked of him." The word *faint* means to "unloose," like an archer would unloose his bowstring, so that it is no longer taut or ready to propel an arrow to the target. When a bowstring does not "twang," it is a useless article, no matter how skilled the archer. God's correction is not intended to discourage us or to make us lose heart but to strengthen us and to ready us for His use.

When we think of Jonah's attempt to flee from God, we realize how feeble such an attempt really was. He naturally headed in the opposite direction from what God wanted, but of course, God knew where he was. Can we successfully run from God? Listen to David's question and his answer in Psalm 139:7-11:

> Whither shall I go from thy spirit? or whither shall I flee from thy presence? If I ascend up into heaven, thou art there: if I make my bed in hell, behold, thou art there. If I take the wings of the morning, and dwell in the uttermost parts of the sea; even there shall thy hand lead me, and thy right hand shall hold me. If I say, Surely the darkness shall cover me; even the night shall be light about me.

An ascent to heaven, a descent to hell, a long journey to some remote part of the vast sea, the cover of darkness — nothing can exclude God, for He alone is omnipresent.

Sometimes, like Jonah, we can be very stubborn and rebellious, not wanting to submit to God's plan for us. We think we know what we want, and regardless of the counsel and admonition of others, we are determined to head in our own chosen way. At those times, we do not enjoy the presence of God; in fact, we try to avoid anything or anyone that would confront us or convict us.

We lose interest in reading God's Word and in praying to Him because our hearts are set on our own way. Jonah who had gone far down into the ship could not say, "In thy presence is fulness of joy" (Ps. 16:11). Can we?

The great wind that God cast into the sea caused a great tempest that threatened to destroy the ship and all on board. A great and terrifying disturbance followed causing misery and unhappiness for Jonah and the sailors. What a picture of the chastening of God. Hebrews 12:11 says, "No chastening for the present seemeth to be joyous, but grievous: nevertheless afterward it yieldeth the peaceable fruit of righteousness unto them which are exercised thereby." The word *grievous* signifies pain and sorrow and is contrasted in the verse with the word *joyous*, which means "with delight." God sends pain and sorrow in His correction so that we might again find His presence delightful.

God Provided Confinement — A Great Fish

"Now the Lord had prepared a great fish to swallow up Jonah" (Jon. 1:17).

God kept Jonah alive three days and three nights in the belly of a fish, and it was in this awful place of confinement that God began to work in Jonah's heart. We can only read Jonah's prayer to God in chapter 2 and imagine the horror of his situation — to be sinking to the bottom of the sea in pitch-black darkness, perhaps unable to move arms or legs, and with weeds wrapped around his head. We think of the panic and desperation of his heart as he thought himself abandoned by God. Just hours before he had been trying to run from God, but now he cried out, "I am cast out of thy sight" (2:4).

God was far from abandoning Jonah, however. He knew exactly where His servant was; He, the Creator, had everything under control, even though it did not look that way to Jonah! Sometimes God needs to confine us or restrict us in order to teach us submission and obedience. We can follow this work of God in Jonah's life by noting two highlights in his prayer of chapter 2.

    1. He cried unto the Lord by reason of his

affliction. "I cried by reason of mine affliction" (Jonah 2:2). It was the affliction of God's correction that stirred Jonah's heart to cry or call urgently to God. We have a tendency, like Jonah, to go our own way in our own strength, whether in deliberate disregard of God's will or in the blindness of our pride, but God's restrictions bring us back on course Psalm 119:67 says, "Before I was afflicted I went astray: but now have I kept thy word." In our affliction we can only acknowledge the truth of Psalm 119:75; "I know, O Lord, that thy judgments are right, and that thou in faithfulness hast afflicted me." Affliction here refers to straitness [constricted to a narrow, tight space]. This is similar in meaning to our English word *straitjacket*, the garment used to restrain a violent person. We don't like straitness or confinement because it makes us realize we have lost control of our own lives. What God seeks to do through such affliction is cause us to acknowledge that He alone has control and that we can trust Him.

2. He remembered the Lord when his soul fainted.

"When my soul fainted within me I remembered the Lord" (Jonah 2:7). The meaning of *fainted* in verse 7 is "shown feeble." How often God must remind us of our feebleness as individuals, as a local church, or as a mission before we remember the Lord and His greatness and turn to Him for strength and enabling. When Samson was in the peak of his strength, he went his own way and set his own course, but after he lost his strength and was captured by the Philistines, it was a different matter. There came a day when, blind and laughed at, Samson called unto the Lord and said, "O Lord God, remember me, I pray thee, and strengthen me" (Judg. 16:28). It was when the children of Israel were trapped by the undefeatable army of Pharaoh behind them and the uncrossable Red Sea before them that they clearly saw their feebleness. This helpless situation was exactly where God wanted them in order to teach them early in their journey that only God provides salvation. Moses said it in these words, "Fear ye not, stand still, and see the salvation of the Lord" (Ex. 14:13).

It is a faithful God that in various ways confines His children in order to teach them to be still and to wait upon Him for direction and supply. When Jonah found himself upon shore again and heard God's word the second time, there was no hesitation. He immediately arose and began the long trip to the city of Nineveh, on the banks of the Tigris River in modern-day Iraq.

God Provided Comfort — A Simple Gourd

"And the Lord prepared a gourd" (Jon. 4:6).

To prepare a gourd is certainly not hard for the One who created the universe, but *why* He did it shows the wonderful tenderness and compassion of God. God made the gourd to grow so that it came up right over Jonah in order to cast a shadow over Jonah's head to deliver him from his grief.

Why was Jonah grieving? After Jonah sounded God's warning to the people of Nineveh, they all repented from the greatest to the least; and when God saw their response, He withheld His judgment. To we who read the account of God's mercy on Nineveh, this is wonderful news indeed; but to Jonah, who had witnessed the abuse the Assyrians inflicted on Israel, it was more than he could take. He would not let go of his desire to see the Assyrians suffer. He would not forgive them for the pain they had caused his people. At first he was displeased, then angry, and then in depression, he wanted his life to end (see Jon. 4:1-3).

We could say that Jonah's grief was self-inflicted, that he brought it on himself because of his wrong attitudes. God could have left Jonah to his misery, but in providing for him, God teaches us this great lesson: *All of God's provisions are provisions of grace, and we deserve none of them.* Psalm 103:10 says, "He hath not dealt with us after our sins; nor rewarded us according to our iniquities." Romans 5:8 says, "But God commendeth his love toward us, in that, while we were yet sinners, Christ died for us."

How easy it might be for us to leave such a stubborn and angry person as Jonah was to his misery and feel justified in doing so! God, however, is called the "God of all comfort" (2 Cor. 1:3), and He is eager to provide the comfort of His love and the security of His care in order to encourage us to trust Him and to respond to Him. This is why He made the gourd to grow up as a shadow over Jonah.

Sometimes when we are in need of comfort like Jonah and Elijah were, we think, "I have brought this grief on myself and I will just have to suffer through it!" Our wrong choices do bring difficulties and sorrows to us that will not just disappear. There may be consequences which we must face, but we do not have to go comfortless. All who have placed their faith in Jesus are indwelt by God's Holy Spirit who was promised by Christ and called the Comforter. In John 14:16 Jesus said, "And I will pray the Father, and he shall give you another Comforter, that he may abide with you for ever." Jesus also promised in John 14:18, "I will not leave you comfortless," or like orphans with no one to turn to who truly cares. Do you need comfort now? God is eager to provide for you, and you do not have to deserve it!

At first Jonah tried to comfort himself by making a shady place to sit, but it was not at all adequate. It is typical of our human nature to try and comfort ourselves when we are miserable and unhappy because of our own wrong behavior or wrong attitudes. Like Jonah, we try to justify our own wrong by blaming others or by pointing out how they have hurt us. Such comfort is fleshly and not at all adequate to meet our needs.

God Provided Reminders — A Worm and a Wind

One of our greatest needs is to remember God. One of God's greatest provisions is that He faithfully reminds us of who He is and what He has done.

First Reminder - A Hungry Worm

"But God prepared a worm" (Jon. 4:7).

God needed to remind Jonah of the temporal nature of things and the eternal nature of souls. When God provided shade through the gourd we read that Jonah was "exceeding glad" (Jon. 4:6) for the gourd. His gladness was in the gourd, not in God who provided the gourd. It is amazing how quickly and how much we can set our heart's affection on things that pass and forget to rejoice in knowing God who gives us all things to enjoy. First Timothy 6:17 says, "Charge them that are rich in this world, that they be not highminded, nor trust in uncertain riches, but in the living God, who giveth us richly all things to enjoy."

Some may say, "It was not fair that God took away the gourd just when Jonah was becoming really happy and content with its shade!" However, God has His own priorities, and He wants us to continue to look in faith to Him as our provider. We are often just like Jonah. When God provides a gourd, we immediately begin to settle down under its shade and plan our entire life around it, as if it were going to be there forever. God never provides for us today so that we will not need to trust Him tomorrow.

There are few life forms more insignificant than the worm, yet God uses it to teach and remind man of the passing nature of earthly life. The worm is not alone; it is in the company of moths, rust, and thieves! This foursome ravages all earthly treasures and comforts of man but is unable to touch heavenly treasures. Matthew 6:19 says that moths and rust continually eat away at our treasures, and thieves are always trying to steal them. Why, then, should we set our hearts upon them?

God used the worm to destroy the gourd so that He might direct Jonah's attention and compassion to the perishing thousands of Nineveh. Our compassion is often misdirected. We become emotional and sentimental about the loss of such temporal things as tools and equipment, money and savings, position and praise, health and comfort. Even those in so-called "full-time work" can easily lose their perspective and become overly concerned about temporal benefits and comforts.

Second Reminder — A Sweltering Wind

"God prepared a vehement east wind" (Jon. 4:8).

Through the wind, God continued to teach Jonah the importance of dealing with wrong attitudes. When God removed the comfort of the gourd and presented the discomfort of the sweltering wind, Jonah's attitude of extreme anger and depression surfaced again. His "exceeding gladness" was only on the surface; still simmering within him was the bitter anger and resentment toward God for being good to Nineveh.

Amazingly enough, Jonah's anger persisted through all of God's dealings with him. Even after he finally obeyed God and traveled to Nineveh, it seems

Jonah was still hoping Nineveh would be destroyed. There is a lesson for us in this. Our location does not determine our attitudes. It is very possible to be serving God in the sense of being in the location He wants us to be, even having traveled thousands of miles to get there, yet to have taken with us ungodly attitudes that simmer in our hearts, waiting to boil over at some provocation. Sometimes God allows a "sweltering east wind" to blow upon us to discomfort us in our spiritual complacency, reminding us that we need to let go of our sinful attitudes and adjust our thinking to the mind of God.

Where does anger toward others come from? As in Jonah's case, we become angry at others when they have hurt us or we imagine they have hurt us. Jonah wanted the Assyrians at Nineveh destroyed. In fact, he wanted to see it happen! That is why he sat under his miserable booth, "till he might see what would become of the city" (Jon. 4:5).

Before we distance ourselves self-righteously from Jonah, let us ask ourselves if we are sitting under a self-made shelter waiting for some failure, disappointment, or judgment to fall on someone who has brought us pain.

Many believers have experienced great pain at the hands of others; all of us have experienced some. However, none of us are right in holding on to our anger or in trying to express it to the one who has hurt us. The man who was hurt more than any other, who experienced more pain of heart and soul than we can ever imagine, cried out from His cross: "Father, forgive them; for they know not what they do" (Luke 23:34).

God Provided Salvation — A City Spared

"And should not I spare Nineveh ...?" (Jon. 4:11)

This was a pointed question to Jonah that brought out three foundational truths which should motivate each of us daily in all we do and say:

1. God does not want any person to be lost — He wanted to spare them. We read in 2 Peter 3:9 that God is "longsuffering to us-ward, not willing that any should perish, but that all should come to repentance." Again, in Ezekiel 33:11 we read, "As I live, saith the Lord God, I have no pleasure in the death of the wicked."

2. God alone can provide salvation to the lost — He used the personal pronoun *I*. God was the only One who could provide salvation for Nineveh. We remember that Sennacherib had built a wall forty to fifty feet high around the city of Nineveh. Today, walls are no protection for a city, but in the days of Nineveh they were a defense that in many cases held off the enemy. Yet, building higher walls could never hold off God's judgment and Jonah was not speaking idle words when he cried, "Yet forty days, and Nineveh shall be overthrown" (Jon. 3:4).

3. God has given us the message of salvation to bring to the lost — He had wanted to use Jonah. The Ninevites were saved from destruction by believing God's words spoken through Jonah.

Unfortunately, the people of Nineveh returned to their wicked ways and the city was eventually destroyed in 612 B.C., perhaps one hundred to two hundred years after Jonah's warning. This account of Nineveh's destruction is vividly told in the book of Nahum, where the author begins his account with the introductory words, "The burden of Nineveh."

Nahum 1:3 is no doubt intended as a reminder of the days of Jonah when God in His long-suffering provided salvation to Nineveh: "The Lord is slow to anger, and great in power."

The lesson is clear: for any who reject the provision of God's salvation, there is no hope of any salvation elsewhere. Nahum 3:19 says, "There is no healing of thy bruise; thy wound is grievous." For Nineveh, there was no hope of a remnant. As in the illustration of Nineveh, it is impossible and unavoidable for the wicked to escape God's judgment outside of the salvation God provides. We follow this truth into the New Testament and the words of Christ in John 3:15 — "That whosoever believeth in him should not perish, but have eternal life."

In conclusion, think back over God's provisions:

God provided a *witness* — How is He asking you to serve Him? There is no greater privilege, in time or eternity.

God provided *correction* — Are you experiencing it? Don't despise it or faint, for God is at work in your life.

God provided *confinement* — It is difficult to realize we do not have control of our lives, but God is in control and will never leave us nor forsake us.

God provided *comfort* — God's comfort is a provision of His grace. You do not have to deserve it.

God provided *reminders* — Thank God for them because they refocus our affection on God and eternal matters.

God provided *salvation* — Have you placed your trust in God or are you simply building higher walls?

Chapter Twenty-Three

ASPECTS OF CONFORMITY

"And be not conformed to this world: but be ye transformed by the renewing of your mind, that ye may prove what is that good, and acceptable, and perfect, will of God" (Rom. 12:2).

Two areas of concern are ever before those in spiritual leadership and should also concern each believer as he takes stock of his own life. Paul introduced these concerns in Romans 12:1-2 by beseeching his readers to choose one and refuse the other. His concern is seen in the words "I beseech you" which can be translated, "I beg of you, please." The two areas of tremendous importance are that we be "acceptable unto God" and that we "be not conformed to this world."

What does it mean to be conformed to this world, and how does it happen to a child of God? There are many aspects of conformity that as individual believers, local churches, and Christian organizations we would be wise to be aware of and alert to. Also, there are various ways of thinking which the world presents to us that are an attempt to weaken our resistance. Some of these aspects and ways of thinking are presented in this chapter in hopes that God would encourage each of us in our desire to live pleasing to Him.

The Uncomfortable Aspect of Pressure

The word *conformed* introduces the aspect of pressure from without. This pressure is intended to shape us according to the views and standards of the world so that instead of desiring solely to be acceptable unto God, we entertain a growing desire to be acceptable to people. It is not easy for us to be scorned or to be thought evil of. It can be frightening and very stressful. We naturally want to be liked and accepted. For this reason it is easy for us to think that it is important for the world to give us its stamp of credibility. It is not wrong if others are pleased when we are pleasing God, but it is wrong to please men at the sacrifice of pleasing God.

At times the pressure to conform is both noticeable and painful, but at other times the pressure is only slightly apparent. Perhaps we are in the most danger when the pressure to conform involves issues of seemingly little consequence or when we fail to realize our growing desire to please men. In Luke 6:26 Jesus said, "Woe unto you, when all men shall speak well of you!" To be spoken well of is not proof that we have conformed to the world, but neither is it an indication of God's blessing! The principle is very clear: it is not possible for the world to be always pleased with our priorities and our behavior. Jesus said in John 15:19, "If ye were of the world, the world would love his own: but because ye are not of the world, but I have chosen you out of the world, therefore the world hateth you." Again in his prayer for us in John 17:14 Jesus said, "And the world hath hated them, because they are not of the world, even as I am not of the world." Because we are in it but not of it, the world hates us.

The world will appear to accept us if we pattern our lives after its system, and this, in a nutshell, is the basic source of the pressure. We must come to grips with what Jesus clearly taught. We are not of the world but have been called out of it.

Although we should always maintain integrity and openness in all we do, we should not seek the approval of this world, and we should not be surprised when the world rejects us or accuses us. To seek to gain the world's acceptance is like a chicken swimming in a pond full of ducks, hoping to go unnoticed! The chicken has conformed to the life-style of the duck, but will never be a duck or be approved by them, though it might be tolerated. The word *conformed* can never be used for an inward change or transformation, so the chicken remains a chicken though it tries to swim with the ducks. If we live acceptably unto God, we simply cannot avoid being the object of the world's hatred. Paul said in 2 Timothy 3:12, "Yea, and all that will live godly in Christ Jesus shall suffer persecution."

The Weakening Aspect of Repetition

The word *conformed* introduces the aspect of a gradual but persistent pressure. Probably very few believers have abandoned their desire to be acceptable to God in favor of becoming like the world as the result of a single choice. Repetition or constant pressure can have an eroding and wearing effect upon us, as in the case of Samson. When Delilah first began to ask Samson to reveal to her the secret of his great strength, he seemed to enjoy making up stories to deceive her. Perhaps, to him, it started out to be a game that he controlled. However, in Judges 16:16-17 we read, "And it came to pass, when she pressed him daily with her words, and urged him, so that his soul was vexed unto death; that he told her all his heart."

The world has one objective—to pour our lives into its mold of ungodliness so our lives will not be pleasing to God. It has many ways to accomplish this goal, and the repetition of these approaches can wear us down. The world's philosophy or way of looking at values begins to affect us by entering into our own thinking processes. Believers sometimes think there is no danger to them in their daily contact with the world's way of thinking. However, if we hear untruths often enough, presented in different ways and by different means, we can begin to believe them and embrace them as guidelines to live by. It is amazing how many sayings of men, some good and some not so good, are quoted as though they were from the Bible itself:

"Cleanliness is next to godliness."

"God helps those who help themselves."

We may accumulate ways of thinking that seem good as guidelines but are not based upon the Word of God. When we fall for these, we place one foot into the world's mold where the conforming process takes place.

The Shaping Aspect of Fashioning

Conformity carries the meaning of "sameness" or "likeness" or "to fashion or shape one thing like another." *The New Testament In Modern English* by J.B. Phillips translates the first part of our verse this way: "Don't let the world around you squeeze you into its own mold." It is wrong thinking on our part to suppose that we should not stand out but should be able to blend into this world's system.

This is exactly the world's objective for us, and

blending is part of the conforming process. The convicting influence of the believer can be diffused if there is little difference between his framework of thinking or manner of life and that of the world about him. Jesus said in Matthew 5:13, "Ye are the salt of the earth: but if the salt have lost his savour, wherewith shall it be salted? it is thenceforth good for nothing..." The question is, Have I become insipid in my testimony because I don't want to stand out as extreme or fanatical? Is my life dull and flat as a convicting force for God and godliness in this world?

The Scriptures point to many who have stood out to the world as ridiculous because they confessed a belief in God and insisted upon obeying Him. One example is Noah, who Hebrews 11:7 says was "warned of God of things not seen as yet." Even though the people of the earth had never seen rain up to that point, Noah began building an ark that would provide salvation during the flood to come.

The Controlling Aspect of Leading

Conformity implies that a standard of thinking and behavior has already been established by the world. Believers are not asked to contribute godliness to those standards but only to fit into the system. For this reason it is dangerous when considering change to adopt the mind-set, "Don't be the first to try new things. Wait until the change is generally acceptable or seen as ordinary; then go ahead." It is amazing how often Christians apply this dangerous principle to areas of entertainment and behavior.

There is a little creature called the lemming that lives in the tundra of the far north. These extremely energetic little animals reach a population peak every four to five years and then begin to look for more room to spread out. However, as they migrate in large numbers, they sometimes scurry blindly over cliffs and into the ocean where they perish. They never pause to ask themselves, *Who is leading me?* or, *Where are they taking me?* They blindly follow the crowd, feeling safe, because instinct has set their course.

Unfortunately, we do not seem as concerned about who is setting the course we are following as we are about who else is following; if the crowd of followers includes people of reputation, we relax our guard and think, *If they are doing it, it must be okay.*

Submitting to the Word of God is our only assurance of staying on a godly course and living lives acceptable unto God. Our complacency is probably our greatest problem. If we are unconcerned that we might conform to this world, our reading of the Word will be casual; but if we realize how easily we can be misled, then our reading takes on a desperate hunger and eager searching. David expressed it this way: "As the hart panteth after the water brooks, so panteth my soul after thee, O God. My soul thirsteth for God, for the living God" (Ps. 42:1-2).

The power of God's Word to expose our thinking and reveal the influence of the world upon it is seen in Hebrews 4:12. "For the word of God ... is a discerner of the thoughts and intents of the heart." Second Timothy 3:16-17 is very explicit in showing that the Word of God is the only help for us if we would live acceptably unto God. "All scripture is given by inspiration of God, and is profitable ... unto all good works."

The Promising Aspect of "Liberty"

Sometimes conformity gives the appearance of freedom from legalism and is appealing because it seems to offer liberty from the bondage of dos and don'ts. However, this world's system has refused the rule of God since its beginning. This is seen clearly in

Cain's attitude of hate toward God and the rebellious attitude of those building the tower of Babel who insisted on doing their own thing in rejection of God's command. Such attitudes represent the greatest degree of bondage!

Because of the appearance of liberty, believers can begin to think that if they say no too much, they are legalistic. The world's system would have believers mistake legalism for the instruction of God's grace. Titus 2:11-12 says, "For the grace of God that bringeth salvation hath appeared to all men, teaching us that, denying ungodliness and worldly lusts, we should live soberly, righteously, and godly, in this present world." In this verse the grace of God is seen as instructing us how to think and how to behave. First, we are instructed to deny or say no to ungodliness and second, we are instructed how to live so as to please God. It is clear that our daily life is to be lived under the direction of God's grace alone with the law, legalism, and fleshly license excluded.

The Convincing Aspect of Persuasion

Conformity involves a change in attitude concerning what is accepted. At one time in the history of the church certain attitudes or behavioral patterns were unacceptable to believers, but with the passing of time and the continued pressure of the world, they came to be considered acceptable. How is it that we have come to accept the unacceptable? We have been persuaded that the things Christians rejected in the past were really okay but they were not acceptable because of the culture of those times. We may make many excuses for our compromising and conforming using this faulty reasoning. Certainly there are many changes in our way of life that have nothing to do with conformity of the world. There have been more scientific and technological changes in the last one hundred years than in the many hundreds of years prior to that and for the most part, we have benefited by these changes. However, there has also been relentless pressure by the world to force believers to accept a standard of morality that expresses the world's rebellion toward God and rejection of God's Word as authority. Notice what Paul wrote to Timothy revealing this stepped-up pressure upon believers: "Now the Spirit speaketh expressly, that in the latter times some shall depart from the faith" (1 Tim. 4:1); "This know also, that in the last days perilous times shall come" (2 Tim. 3:1); "For the time will come when they will not endure sound doctrine" (2 Tim. 4:3).

Paul's encouragement to remain constant and not be deceived into conformity is clearly given in 2 Timothy 3:13-14. "But evil men and seducers shall wax worse and worse, deceiving, and being deceived. But continue thou in the things which thou hast learned and hast been assured of." The words *worse and worse* indicate in which direction the world's system is headed, while the word *continue* indicates that the believer is to remain steadfast and unmovable in godliness.

The world's digression away from God and godliness is said to be deceiving, so it may appear simply as a change brought about by time or culture. Conformity to this downward, sliding scale of morality happens to us as we tire of resisting ungodly change and begin to find it less and less offensive.

The Threatening Aspect of Loss

Not to conform carries with it the threat of losing something. Faced with this possibility, we become anxious and sometimes make compromises that seem to have a promise of continued prosperity. We allow ourselves to be deceived by the thinking that unless we make adjustments to our policies and standards, we lose people that might otherwise join our ranks. If people tell us that our dress standard is too strict for today's world or that our music is too conservative, we feel that we must lighten up in order to encompass a wider spectrum of people.

When God shows us we should make alterations to our standards or requirements, we should do so, but when we feel pressured by men to change or lose out, we should hold fast to what we know to do. The trend of Christian organizations to drop requirements and lower standards appears to indicate that God never seems to encourage us to raise our standards but always to lower them!

All too readily we forget the story of how God deliberately reduced Gideon's fighting men from over thirty thousand to a mere three hundred! God has never been concerned with numbers or quantity because He is the One who accomplishes His own purposes, using lives yielded to Him. He said to Gideon, "By the three hundred men that lapped will I save you" (Judg. 7:7). Perhaps there were some who suggested to Gideon that if he simply lightened up in his qualifications, he would easily have thousands of soldiers instead of just hundreds to send into battle.

The Drawing Aspect of Attraction

Conformity implies attraction. The world attracts the unsuspecting believer into its mold, using myriad enticements. It may be the promise of prosperity, pleasure, or power, but the attraction creates a growing desire when yielded to. Conformity can be outwardly drastic in its result such as in the case of Demas, who responded to the world like a nail to a magnet. Paul wrote, "Demas hath forsaken me, having loved this present world" (2 Tim. 4:10). On the other hand, conformity can be less obvious on the outside but nonetheless devastating, robbing the believer of the joy of worshiping God and the hunger for His Word. Isn't it sobering to realize that we could fall in love with this world and its ungodliness? Demas had been one of Paul's trusted helpers, but he abandoned Paul and let him down when he needed him most because he had set his affection on the spirit of the age in which he lived.

We are mistaken if we have the attitude, "What is evil will be repulsive to the child of God." If this were true, why would John write "Love not the world, neither the things that are in the world" (1 John 2:15)? We must change our thinking in this and be alert — the world is not always unattractive on the surface; in fact, it can exert tremendous pull on our fleshly senses and desires as brought out in the words of 1 John 2:16 "...the lust of the flesh, and the lust of the eyes, and the pride of life."

The Disarming Aspect of Deceit

It is wrong to conclude that we do not have the power to keep from conforming. If we choose this way of thinking, it is like surrendering arms to an already defeated foe.

The world cannot conform us without our consent. Romans 12:2 clearly shows that we have a choice by giving the command, "Be not conformed to this world." This is something to be obeyed, and it calls for a response on the part of the believer. Indeed, the world's attraction can be great and its enticements deceitful and full of treachery. It may seem overwhelming in its bullying and frightful in its threats. Still we have a choice because of our identification with Christ our Savior in His death, burial, and resurrection. We are now free to live "acceptable unto God." Romans 6:19 says, "For as ye have yielded your members servants to uncleanness and to iniquity unto iniquity; even so now yield your members servants to righteousness unto holiness."

Why do we make the wrong choices and conform? The main reason is that we do not focus our hearts' affection upon God. In Colossians 3:1-2 we read, "If ye then be risen with Christ, seek those things which are above, where Christ sitteth on the right hand of God. Set your affection on things above, not on things on the earth." A mouse at the foot of a trap is overwhelmed by the tangy smell of sharp cheese and will make a poor choice because of where he is setting his affection.

The "Harmless" Aspect of Little Things

Little compromises are more effective for the world and devastating for us than the possibility of one big surrender. This is simply because we cannot see the harm in little things. Our way of thinking may be "Don't be so picky" or "Don't make a mountain out of a molehill!" Conformity suggests that we do not always have a clear sense of the danger we are in. Solomon, the wisest of men, was conformed to his world like a soft chunk of clay by the little changes in his life and kingdom. We read that he "loved many strange women" (1 Kings 11:1) and no doubt, each relationship seemed so right to him. However, when Solomon was old, "his wives turned away his heart after other gods" (1 Kings 11:4). The word *turned* means "to incline or lean." As Solomon was gathering silver, linen, yarn, horses from Egypt, and women from all over, he was growing increasingly unaware of the inclination of his heart away from God and toward the world. The world has a way of making things seem logical, progressive, and harmless. It tells us, "Don't make mountains out of molehills," and we forget that enough molehills will make a mountain. When the first horse from Egypt pranced into Jerusalem, it was just a molehill, but when the kingdom of Israel was divided after Solomon's reign, it was a mountain!

Solomon's protection against conformity was not his own wisdom. As pride and self-importance entered into his thinking, he became easy prey for the world. Likewise our protection against conformity to the world is not our own sense of right and wrong; nor is it other people's sense of right and wrong. Our confidence must be solely in God, and our hearts' submission must be only to His Word.

A Renewed Mind

"Be ye transformed by the renewing of your mind." This portion of Romans 12:2 emphasizes the faithfulness of God's Holy Spirit in speaking to our hearts through God's Word, showing us where our thinking needs to be brought into submission so that our behavior expresses not the ungodly attitudes of the world but the life of Christ. We have no other source whereby we can be kept from conformity to this world and continue to live acceptably unto God.

Chapter Twenty-Four

KEEP IT SIMPLE!

"Looking unto Jesus the author and
finisher of our faith" (Heb. 12:2).

How quickly we are distracted from simplicity! We have all observed a room, a table, perhaps a dresser top that is cluttered. It is hard to find things and easy to lose things in the midst of clutter. We probably just have too much stuff, or we simply don't take the time to keep things in order. Our spiritual lives can also become cluttered with false hopes and fleshly determinations. These things should be cleaned out and discarded. Hebrews 12:2 focuses our attention on our single source of life: "Looking unto Jesus the author and finisher of our faith." From beginning to end, Jesus Christ is all you need!

Simplicity in Confidence

One of the greatest dangers that faces believers is a

subtle shift of confidence from the Lord Jesus Christ as the supplier of all our needs and the source of all our strength to some other much-advertised but nonetheless feeble support system of man.

When David, in 1 Samuel 17:38-40, appeared before King Saul prepared in his heart to do battle with Goliath, it is striking that Saul offered him his own armor! What a ponderous, cumbersome, heavy outfit of brass and mail! Little good it had done Saul! It had not fortified him to go out to meet the giant! Why, then, should he offer it to David? This is how the worldly wise are. They will offer help that cannot help. They will throw to a drowning man a line that is frayed and rotten and breaks even as it is seized! King Saul knew nothing of the simple confidence in God that had become reality to the young shepherd boy. Can you see David staggering toward the tent door under the weight of Saul's armor? We all find ourselves at times trying to "go out with Saul's armor." We must be quick to realize the fallacy of this as David did. His words to Saul in 1 Samuel 17:39 are our testimony: "I cannot go with these; for I have not proved them." His choice of five smooth stones did not mean that five smooth stones were now the answer to all life's problems! It was not stones David had proved, but God Himself. With the boldness of a lion, he said to Goliath, "I come to thee in the name of the Lord!" (v. 45).

There are times for each of us as Christian soldiers when we become physically, emotionally, and spiritually weary due to the unavoidable strains and stresses of fighting in a spiritual battle. We struggle with a lack of accomplishment, painful memories of our past, and haunting doubts about our qualifications to do our job. At this point, the ENEMY is quick to try to steer our confidence away from God and onto false hopes.

"What you need to do is enroll in this seminar or in

these courses in University and rethink your goals and objectives." Regrettably, many who follow this advice never return to their posts again but somehow find that their goals have changed.

Another voice insists, "You must rethink the past and get in touch with that part of yourself that is hurting." Sadly, many times this turns out to be a lifelong pursuit, and it demands so much attention that it is impossible to continue in ministry.

Yet another voice tells us, "Your problems stem from your poor self-esteem." What we need, they claim, is to gain self-worth and self-respect. All too often when people emerge from this lengthy introspection, they are tragically worth so much that they cannot seem to return contentedly to the service where they can hope for little praise and perhaps only ridicule.

The world and humanism despises simplicity of faith in Jesus Christ. He alone is the answer to our basic need to be brought into a right relationship with the Creator God, and He is the answer to all our needs as weak human beings.

When God declared to Abraham and Sarah that they would produce a son, it seemed such an impossibility to Sarah that she laughed. By unbelief she complicated a very simple promise. She began to question how God's promise could be possible at her advanced age. At this point in Genesis 18:14, God asked Abraham this question, which He directs to each of us, regardless of our unique need: "Is anything too hard for the Lord?"

Should we depend upon courses and seminars to refocus our spiritual goals? Should we trust in our memory and psychology to work forgiveness in our lives toward those who have hurt us? Should we seek to gain "self-anything" when God is everything?

According to how we answer the question of

Genesis 18:14, we will disclose where our confidence really is. We have no need that He cannot answer, but do we know how to look to Him for the help we need? Jesus said in John 10:10, "I am come that they might have life, and that they might have it more abundantly." Abundant life is life marked with great spiritual plenty. Spiritual drought or spiritual plenty is a direct result of where our source of life truly is. When our delight is in the Lord, then Psalm 1:3 is true for us: "And he shall be like a tree planted by the rivers of water, that bringeth forth his fruit in his season; his leaf also shall not wither; and whatsoever he doeth shall prosper."

A tree can be in a parched and dry land, but if its roots have found a water supply, the tree will flourish despite the elements. It is not so much your present circumstances or past hurts that determine the quality of your life; the question is one of roots. Are you drawing from the unlimited supply of life in Christ Jesus?

Simplicity in Acceptance

The foundation of our service and worship of God is the knowledge that we are fully and completely accepted by Him.

When a boy is eager to please his father but finds that he cannot because his father is demanding and simply will not be pleased, there begins a very frustrating relationship that is never truly enjoyable or close. This painful relationship often continues through adolescence and adversely affects the son's attitudes toward his heavenly Father.

While as human parents we can fail and hurt our children in not accepting them, God fully and without reservation accepts all who place their trust in His perfect Son.

We are accepted by God not because of who we are or what we have done, but because of who Jesus Christ is and what He has done on our behalf. For this reason we cannot possibly be any more accepted by God in the future than we are just now as we read these words found in Ephesians 1:6. "To the praise and glory of his grace, wherein he hath made us accepted in the beloved."

However, although our acceptance is established, we complicate and confuse things when we live by our feelings. We feel of such little worth that we strive to prove to God and our co-workers that we are valuable. After all, aren't we getting up early and staying up late? Don't we fall into bed exhausted each night? Don't we keep on working when we feel tired and perhaps even sick with malaria?

What is really behind our strivings to be accepted? It is because of the pride of our hearts that we like to work things out on our own. There is nothing that confuses and complicates more than human effort. Flesh effort detracts immediately from the simplicity found in Christ and focuses instead on the complexity of a system of works. At first we love the prospect of harnessing ourselves to a load of things to do in order to please God. It makes us feel so good to think that if we do all these things, God will be pleased with us and the needs in our lives will be straightened out. Pulling a heavy load of works at first makes us feel good about ourselves; however, we do not pull the load long before our needs and weaknesses are magnified and we become discouraged. Often at the point of seeing our failure we throw even more on the wagon of works and pile the load still higher, partly to punish ourselves for failure and partly to prove we can do it. We need not do either, for our acceptance with God is already accomplished.

Simplicity in Dealing With Sin

Our relationship and our fellowship with God is based on our acceptance in Christ. Although we know our relationship with God can never be altered, we know also that our fellowship with Him can be broken by sin that we allow into our lives. God has made a very simple provision for us when sin has broken our fellowship with Him. It is the wonderful promise of 1 John 1:9 that has comforted saints for many centuries. "If we confess our sins, he is faithful and just to forgive us our sins, and to cleanse us from all unrighteousness."

However, simplicity threatens those who are fearful of the truth! Often complexity and confusion are a defense mechanism designed to prevent full exposure to the naked truth of our need to humble ourselves before God. We deliberately allow things to become complicated as a smoke screen to obscure our sinful thoughts or behavior so that we do not have to deal with our wrong. John 3:20 says, "For everyone that doeth evil hateth the light, neither cometh to the light, lest his deeds should be reproved."

In our attempt to cloud the issue of our sin and the need to confess that sin before God, we choose many confusing avenues:

    1. We choose to do nothing about it. We allow our insensitivity to sin to control our thoughts and refuse to be affected by the prompting of the Holy Spirit. We may speak a harsh word of criticism toward our wife, husband, or co-worker and simply continue on with what we're doing without a second thought of the devastation we've caused or the confusion and spiritual darkness we are walking in.

    2. We escape behind tiredness and

exhaustion. Often because sin is troubling us, we do feel tired. However, we complicate our lives by trying to block out our need to seek forgiveness with sleeping. We think a good night's rest will make us feel better and in some ways, we actually might require rest; however, we would certainly rest a lot better if we humbled ourselves first!

3. We presume upon God's grace and character by thinking we can take our time getting things sorted out. We think, "God will forgive me anyway, so it doesn't really matter if I stay out of fellowship for a while." However, we run a real risk of increasing the confusion of our hearts and minds by becoming hardened to sin and unable to respond readily to God's prompting.

4. We blatantly refuse to seek forgiveness, enjoying our hardness, anger, bitterness, or discouragement. We simply do not want to get things cleared up with God and others. On the contrary, our hearts and minds are bent on hurting others. Our spiritual enemy has us where he wants us when we provide such ground for him to work confusion and complication in our lives.

5. We excuse ourselves. If only we could see the dense woods of confusion we enter when we begin to blame others for our sin or when we try to redefine sin as something more acceptable. Someone said, "We each have endless capacity for self-deception and are notoriously biased in our own favor." Do any of these excuses sound familiar to you?

- "I'm upset with you."
- "I'm just out of sorts today."
- "I've had a hard day."

- "I'm just tired, that's all."
- "You made me angry."

6. We give way to guilt, condemnation, discouragement, and bad feelings. We can be so low in spirit that we have to reach up to touch bottom, yet never confess our sin to God. Judas felt so low he committed suicide, yet he never repented of his sin. The flesh always wants to make things right. In the case of sin, the flesh will try to make amends by penance, which means "an act of self-abasement, mortification or devotion." We enter a confusing jungle of feeling sorry for ourselves in an attempt to reach a point where we have suffered enough.

Simplicity in Wisdom

Wisdom is essential to us each day we live. There are so many decisions to ponder, so many choices to make, and so many temptations to avoid. Where shall we turn to know what to do and how to think?

Many books cram the shelves of bookstores with titles which catch the eye and attention of weary saints in need of making wise decisions. Yet comparatively few of these books actually direct the saint simply and solely to Jesus Christ. Many of these works lead the reader away from simplicity in Christ and into philosophy and the wisdom of man

We should remember that any spiritual helps written by man are good only if they direct our hearts and minds to God and to His Word. Paul wrote a warning to the Colossians that applies very well to us today: "Beware lest any man spoil you through philosophy and vain deceit, after the tradition of men, after the rudiments of the world, and not after Christ" (Col 2:8).

Many who promote philosophy would say that it is

too simplistic merely to "trust in Christ." However, we must always keep before us, not *man's* opinions, but what God says, and this is what He says in Colossians 2:6: "As ye have therefore received Christ Jesus the Lord, so walk ye in him."

When we received Christ Jesus the Lord, we simply and solely trusted in Him as God's provision for our need of a Savior. We are instructed to walk or to live our lives day by day exactly the same way — by trusting in Christ to direct our steps. Consider what God has provided for us in His Son, "In whom are hid all the treasures of wisdom and knowledge" (Col. 2:3), "For in him dwelleth all the fulness of the Godhead bodily" (Col. 2:9). Regardless of what the scholars of the world tell us, we need nothing more than what we already have, or perhaps it would be better to say, we need *no one other than who we already have.* Colossians 2:10 confirms this truth by saying, "And ye are complete in him."

How complete are we in Christ? Are we "full to capacity" so that there is no room for anything else? If we are, why should we seek wisdom for life's decisions from the world's wise men? According to 1 Corinthians 1:30, wisdom is in Jesus Christ Himself: "But of him are ye in Christ Jesus, who of God is made unto us wisdom."

Simplicity in Relationships

In every earthly relationship there are times when we differ in opinion or viewpoint with those close to us — husbands and wives, parents and children, or co-workers.

Perhaps you can identify with me when I say that I have been amazed how quickly a conversation can become complicated and the issues confused. On those occasions I have asked myself, *How did this happen?*

How did everything get so complicated and mixed up?
One of the things I naturally want to do is to consider the faults of the other person. For example, it is easy to think that they do not understand me and did not even try. It is not hard to discover ways that they were unreasonable or did not really listen to what I was saying. Of course, I can also find faults of my own that led to the confusion, but it is impossible to sort out all the confusion so that each of us receives the blame that is due.

Much study and analysis has been done and many conclusions have been reached concerning why people do not get along. It is suggested that it is because of incompatibility, personality differences, or conflicting temperaments.

I have settled it in my own heart, however, that this is not the way to a clear understanding of why our earthly relationships become strained. Simplicity and understanding is in Christ, while complexity and confusion occur whenever we take our eyes from Him.

Whenever I have contributed to confusion in my relationship with my wife, children, or co-workers, it is because my focus has been upon myself, and what has been important to me is that I be understood and appreciated. However, if my heart's desire is that Christ be glorified in my relationships and that His will and purposes be known and obeyed, then confusion cannot enter or continue.

What is required is that I walk humbly before God and others. This is simplicity. First Corinthians 14:33 gives us a scriptural principle that serves as a flashing red stoplight whenever we find our relationships departing from simplicity: "For God is not the author of confusion, but of peace."

The word *confusion* speaks of a state of disorder, instability, and disturbance, while the word *peace* emphasizes a harmonious relationship resulting in rest and contentment.

God authored peace in our relationships by establishing unity found only in His Spirit. It is clear that unity is not based on personality, compatibility, or temperaments, but on the work of the Spirit. Our responsibility is only to keep it by seeking Christ's glory and purposes, "endeavouring to keep the unity of the Spirit in the bond of peace" (Eph. 4:3).

Scripture Index

Chapter 1
Acts 13:50 16
1 Corinthians 13 16
2 Corinthians 11:27 15
2 Corinthians 11:33 15
Daniel 7:25 12
Ecclesiastes 3:1 18
Galatians 6:9 18
Hebrews 13:5 17
Iasiah 40:31 18
Isaiah 14:14 12
Isaiah 14:15 13
Isaiah 40:28 18
Isaiah 50:4 11
Isaiah 61:10 9
Isiah 50:4 7
John 4:6 14
1 Kings 19:10,14 13
1 Kings 19:18 13
Matthew 16:18 13
Philippians 2:4 14
Psalms 95:7 13
1 Samuel 23:16 17
2 Samuel 17:1-2 17

Chapter 2
1 Corinthians 4:7 24
Galatians 5:26 23
Jeremiah 45:5 19
John 21:19-22 25
3 John 9-11 21
Luke 9:46 23
Luke 22:24 23
Mark 10:35-45 24
Mark 9:33-37 23
Matthew 18:1 23
Numbers 12:1-2 22
Philippians 2:7 25
Philippians 4:2 25
1 Samuel 18:5-9 20

Chapter 3
1 Corinthians 9:24 33
1 Corinthians 9:25 27
Galatians 6:17 28
Hebrews 10:24 30
Hebrews 12:1-2 31
Matthew 25:21 33
Philippians 4:11-13 29

Chapter 4
Galatians 4:16 38
1 Peter 5:2 38
1 Peter 5:2-3 37
Psalms 78:70-72 35

Chapter 5
Acts 9:15-16 43
Ephesians 1:6 48
Ephesians 4:31-32 47
Genesis 34 41
Genesis 49:5,7 42
Hebrews 12:15 42
Isaiah 53:4 47
Isaiah 55:7 47
Joel 2:25 44

Scripture Index

John 10:10 43
John 16:13 49
John 4:16-18 45
John 4:28-29 46
John 8:1-11 48
1 John 1:9 46
Luke 15:17 44
Luke 8:43-48 44
Mark 14:36 47
Nehemiah 9:17 47
Romans 12:19 46
Romans 8:22 40
Titus 2:1-5 42

Chapter 6
Colossians 3:23 55
1 Corinthians 15:58 50
1 Corinthians 4:1-2 52
2 Corinthians 8:12 51
Daniel 6:4 53
John 6:9 51
Luke 16:10 54
Mark 12:41-44 52
Matthew 25:21 51
Nehemiah 9:8 50
Proverbs 28:20 50
Psalms 12:1 55
Revelation 2:13 51
Titus 1:7 54

Chapter 7
1 Corinthians 10:14 59
1 Corinthians 6:18 59
Genesis 39:12 59
Habakkuk 1:13 60
Hebrews 12:15 58
Isaiah 52:11 57

1 John 1:9 60
Joshua 7:21 58
Jude 23 58
2 Kings 5 60
Mark 15:34 60
Romans 12:9 58
1 Timothy 6:11 59
2 Timothy 2:21 57
2 Timothy 2:22 59

Chapter 8
Hebrews 11:6 63
John 21:21-22 63
John 4:34 62
Luke 12:21 62
Proverbs 13:19 61
2 Timothy 4:7 63

Chapter 9
Colossians 4:9-11 70
2 Corinthians 1:3-4 69
2 Corinthians 7:5-6 70
Isaiah 42:3 67
John 13:15 66
John 14:1 66
Psalms 17:7 68
Psalms 25:6 68
Psalms 26:3 69
Psalms 27:14 65
Psalms 40:10 69
Psalms 40:11-12 69
Romans 5:5 70
1 Samuel 23:16 67

Chapter 10
Exodus 3:2 77
James 5:17 73

Philippians 2:21 73
Psalms 107:27-29........78
Psalms 115:1 72
Romans 8:1 78

Chapter 11
  Acts 7:54-60................83
  1 Corinthians
    15:54-57 83
  Genesis 37:13...............82
  Hebrews 11:36-38.......83
  John 4:34......................82
  John 15:4......................84
  Judges 16:30 83
  1 Kings 18:21...............73
  1 Kings 18:27...............73
  1 Kings 18:36...............76
  1 Kings 19:10...............76
  1 Kings 18:39...............73
  1 Kings 18:40...............74
  1 Kings 19:10...............79
  1 Kings 19:11...............78
  1 Kings 19:15...............79
  1 Kings 19:18...............79
  1 Kings 19:2.................74
  1 Kings 19:5-8 75
  1 Kings 19:7.................77
  1 Kings 19:8-10 75
  1 Kings 21:20...............80
  1 Kings 21:23...............80
  Revelation 2:10............83
  Romans 6:6,12,14 84
  2 Timothy 2:4 81

Chapter 12
  1 Corinthians 1:10........92
  Ephesians 4:3 92

Galatians 5:13-15........86
Mark 3:24-25 90
Philippians 2:2 89
Proverbs 13:10............89
Proverbs 18:15............88
Proverbs 22:10............90
Proverbs 23:12............88
Proverbs 24:6..............89
Proverbs 27:17............87
Proverbs 28:25............90
Proverbs 6:16-19.........91
1 Samuel 18:7 91

Chapter 13
  1 Corinthians 2:1.........99
  1 Corinthians 2:4-5 99
  1 Corinthians 8:1.........96
  1 Samuel 16:7 94
  2 Chronicles 22:9........93
  2 Chronicles 23:3........94
  2 Chronicles 24:1-2.....93
  2 Chronicles 24:15......93
  2 Chronicles
    24:17-18....................93
  2 Chronicles 24:22......94
  2 Chronicles 24:4........97
  Hebrews 4:12 95
  James 1:21-22 96
  John 16:13...................95
  Philippians 2:13 98
  Proverbs 3:5 96
  Psalms 127:1 99
  Romans 10:14 96

Chapter 14
  Colossians 1:17..........104
  Hebrews 13:5-6.........105

Scripture Index

Isaiah 49:15-16 105
Isaiah 55:8-9 106
Isaiah 55:9 106
Jeremiah 29:11 101
Lamentations
  3:22-23 104
Luke 12:6-7 103
1 Peter 5:7 102
Philippians 1:6 102
Psalms 92:5 107
Psalms 104:34 107
Psalms 139:12 106
Psalms 13:1-2 105
Psalms 45:5 103
Psalms 92:5 ....100, 106
Romans 11:33 107
Romans 11:33-34 107
Romans 8:38-39 102

Chapter 15

1 Corinthians 12:21 ...111
1 Thessalonians 5:6 ...110
2 Timothy 2:2 113
Deuteronomy 3:28 114
Isaiah 42:3 114
Isaiah 54:2 114
Mark 3:25 112
Philippians 2:3 112
Philippians 2:3-4 112
Proverbs 24:30-34 108
Revelation 3:1 110
Revelation 3:2
  ....108, 109, 115
Revelation 3:3 112

Chapter 16

1 Thessalonians 2:4 ...120

1 Timothy 6:11 125
2 Corinthians
  12:20 ....121, 125
2 Timothy 2:22 125
Colossians 3:8 121
Ephesians 4:31 121
Ephesians 4:32 124
Ephesians 6:19-20 120
Galatians 6:1 124
Genesis 4:5 123
Genesis 4:8 123
James 1:19-20 116
Numbers 20:10 121
Proverbs 14:29 122
Proverbs 15:1 122
Proverbs 15:18 122
Proverbs 16:27-28 125
Proverbs 16:32 122
Proverbs 18:13 119
Proverbs 28:1 120
Proverbs 8:33 118
Psalms 106:32-33 120
Psalms 141:3 116
Romans 6:12-13 122

Chapter 17

2 Timothy 4:3-4 132
2 Timothy 4:5 132
Deuteronomy
  15:16-17 133
Genesis 13:10 131
Genesis 13:14 131
Genesis 1:28 129
Genesis 2:17 129
Genesis 1:31 129
Genesis 39:10 134
Genesis 3:4 130

Genesis 3:6.................130
Job 12:11....................128
Job 31:1......................134
Nehemiah 2:17..........127
Nehemiah 7:3.............134
Proverbs 20:12...........129
Proverbs 2:1-5............133
Psalms 101:3..............134

Chapter 18
Ephesians 4:19...........138
Galatians 6:7..............142
Hebrews 13:15...........142
Hebrews 4:13.............141
1 John 1:9...................141
2 Kings 5:20...............136
2 Kings 5:21...............137
2 Kings 5:22...............138
2 Kings 5:23...............139
2 Kings 5:25...............140
2 Kings 5:26...............141
2 Kings 5:27...............141
Luke 12:15.................137
Numbers 32:23..........141
1 Peter 4:7..................141
2 Peter 3:11................141
Proverbs 6:18.............137
Proverbs 15:27...........136
Psalms 73:17..............140
Psalms 73:3................139
Psalms 73...................139
Romans 5:1-2.............141
2 Timothy 2:22..........137

Chapter 19
Acts 12:21-23.............145
1 Corinthians 10:14...145

2 Corinthians 6:17.....146
Ephesians 4:31-32.....148
Habakkuk 1:13..........146
James 3:17........143, 149
John 12:25..................145
1 John 3:2-3...............148
1 John 4:20.................148
Mark 12:30.................145
Matthew 6:32-33.......145
1 Peter 1:22................148
Proverbs 20:11...........146
Psalms 12:6................144
Psalms 19:8................144
Psalms 49:16-18........149
Revelation 19:15.......147
Romans 1:23..............145
1 Samuel 14:24-29....144
1 Timothy 5:22.........149

Chapter 20
1 Corinthians 3:3........155
Ephesians 4:3.............154
Galatians 5:19-21......155
Genesis 13:8...............150
Genesis 13:9...............156
James 3:16.................155
3 John 9-10................155
Nehemiah 4:3............155
Proverbs 10:12...........151
Proverbs 10:19...........154
Proverbs 13:10...........152
Proverbs 15:18...........151
Proverbs 16:28...........152
Proverbs 18:6.............153
Proverbs 20:19...........153
Proverbs 22:10...........154
Proverbs 25:8.............154

Scripture Index

Proverbs 26:20-21.....153
Proverbs 28:25..........152

Chapter 21
Acts 5:40-42...............162
Colossians 3:13..........162
Colossians 3:15..........157
1 Corinthians 12:21-22..................159
1 Corinthians 15:58...160
1 Corinthians 1:11.....161
1 Corinthians 1:30.....161
1 Corinthians 1:4-5 ...160
1 Corinthians 1:8.......161
1 Corinthians 3:1.......161
1 Corinthians 3:6.......159
1 Corinthians 5:1.......161
1 Corinthinas 3:9.......161
1 Corinthinas 6:11.....161
1 Corinthinas 6:7.......161
Ephesians 1:15,16.....162
Ephesins 5:20............160
Matthew 18:21..........162
Matthew 18:22..........162
Matthew 5:24............157
Matthew 6:33............158
Romans 1:8.......157, 158
1 Thessalonians 4:16-17.....................158

Chapter 22
2 Corinthians 1:3.......173
Exodus 14:13............172
Ezekiel 33:11............177
Hebrews 12:11..........170
Hebrews 12:5-6.........168
John 14:16.................173

John 14:18.................173
John 3:15...................178
Jonah 1:1....................164
Jonah 1:17.................170
Jonah 1:2-3................165
Jonah 1:4...................166
Jonah 2:4...................170
Jonah 2:7...................171
Jonah 3:4...........165, 177
Jonah 4:1-3................173
Jonah 4:11.................176
Jonah 4:5...................176
Jonah 4:6...................172
Jonah 4:7...................174
Jonah 4:8...................175
Judges 16:28..............172
2 Kings 14:25............165
2 Kings 18:11............167
2 Kings 18:30............167
Luke 23:34................176
Mark 4:41..................166
Matthew 6:19............175
Nahum 1:3.................177
Nahum 3:19...............178
2 Peter 3:9.................177
Proverbs 30:4............166
Proverbs 3:11-12........168
Psalms 103:10...........173
Psalms 104:3.............166
Psalms 119:67...........171
Psalms 119:75...........171
Psalms 139:7-11........169
Psalms 16:11.............169
Psalms 68:19.............164
Revelation 22:3.........166
Romans 5:8................173
1 Timothy 6:17.........174

Chapter 23

Colossians 3:1-2........189
Hebrews 11:7............183
Hebrews 4:12............184
Johhn 17:14...............180
John 15:19..................180
1 John 2:15.................188
1 John 2:16.................188
Judges 16:16-17........181
Judges 7:7 187
1 Kings 11:1...............189
1 Kings 11:4...............189
Luke 6:26....................180
Matthew 5:13............183
Psalms 42:1-2............184
Romans
   12:2 ....179, 188, 190
Romans 6:19 189
1 Timothy 4:1 186
2 Timothy 3:1 186
2 Timothy 3:12 181
2 Timothy 3:13-14 186
2 Timothy 3:16-17 184
2 Timothy 4:10 188
2 Timothy 4:3 186
Titus 2:11-12..............185

Ephesians 4:3 201
Genesis 18:14............193
Hebrews 12:2............191
John 10:10.................194
John 3:20....................196
1John 1:9....................196
Psalms 1:3.................194
1 Samuel 17:39 192
1 Samuel 17:45 192

Chapter 24

Colossians 2:10.........199
Colossians 2:3............199
Colossians 2:6...........199
Colossians 2:8...........198
Colossians 2:9...........199
1 Corinthians
   14:33 200
1 Corinthians 1:30.....199
Ephesians 1:6............195

Scripture Index

A Word in Season